FAITH
FOR THE
TIMES

FAITH FOR THE TIMES

Studies in the Prophecy of Isaiah
Chapters 40 to 66

Part I   **THE PROMISE OF DELIVERANCE**

ALAN REDPATH

Fleming H. Revell Company
Old Tappan, New Jersey

All Scripture quotations in this publication are from the *King James Version of the Bible*.

Library of Congress Cataloging in Publication Data

Redpath, Alan.
Faith for the times.

CONTENTS: pt. 1. The promise of deliverance.
1. Bible. O. T. Isaiah XL–LXVI—Sermons.
2. Sermons, American. I. Title.
BS1520.R4   224'.1   72–4621
ISBN 0–8007–0550–5

Contents

Foreword

Alan Redpath, superb Bible expositor and competent evangelist, has done the evangelical world a great service by giving us *The Faith for the Times*. In his incisive, penetrating style he has taken the second part of Isaiah's classic prophecy and brought out things new and old. His treatment of the prophet's utterances possesses a startling freshness, as current as the newspaper columnists of today, yet with a deep, spiritual tone never seen in our daily journals.

He enforces upon our minds that the Bible is relevant to today's problems and needs. He sees the problems of nations as a larger projection of man's personal problems. He gives answers to questions modern man is asking, and he does it with the Word of God as his basis.

This master preacher in *Faith for the Times* demonstrates that he writes as well as he speaks. But best of all, his comments are not of his own manufacture, but are given in the "spirit of truth" to illuminate the eternal truths of the Word of God.

BILLY GRAHAM

Preface

The contents of this volume originally were the basis of a series of messages given from the pulpit of Moody Church, Chicago. They were preached at a time when we, and many other churches in that city, were preparing for a visit from Dr. Billy Graham for a city-wide campaign. This was an event for which I had worked and prayed for years with the burden on my heart that the real effectiveness of an evangelistic crusade would depend upon a breath of true revival in the lives of Christian people in Chicago.

In revising the material for publication I have deliberately refrained from amendment, except when necessary to omit local detail, and I have been more than encouraged to discover that the faith for the times *then* is exactly the faith demanded for today. The world situation has not improved one little bit; rather it has deteriorated. As the years have gone by and my work is no longer confined to a local pastorate, but involves me in visits to many countries, I have become more than ever convinced of the fact that the sovereignty of God is a tremendous reality in the world of today, which is rapidly heading for judgment, yet from which He is still calling a people to His Name.

It is my hope and prayer that this volume may have a small place in the mind of God for recalling Christian people to a firm conviction in His sovereignty, and a personal responsibility to spread abroad the message of His redeeming power.

ALAN REDPATH

Willow Beck Cottage,
Capernwray Hall,
Carnforth,
Lancashire, England.

FAITH
FOR THE
TIMES

1

Isaiah 40:1–12

Grounds for Confidence

... lift up thy voice with strength; lift it up, be not afraid; say unto the cities of Judah, Behold your God! (Isaiah 40:9)

As we consider the closing chapters of the Book of Isaiah, many will know that this prophecy as a whole is delivered in three sections. The first is in chapters 1 to 35 and is prophetic, the theme being one of condemnation; the second section is from chapters 36 to 39, and is historic, the theme being confiscation; the third section is from chapters 40 to 66 and is messianic, and the theme is consolation.

In the last century and a half quite a weight of scholarship has come out against the unity of this prophecy, declaring that the closing section of it must have been given by someone other than Isaiah. Among the reasons stated for this is that it was apparent that the writer is saying something to a time which is considerably future to that in which Isaiah lived, and therefore how could he know anything about it? Furthermore, as there is such a change in the theme, how could the same man have written all?

I am not entering into the controversy more than to say that those of us who believe in the inspiration and authority of the Holy Spirit have no question in our mind about the unity of this prophecy. When we recognize that prophecy is not merely forthtelling but foretelling, when it has always the element of

13

prediction of the future, there is no problem to the reader who accepts the authority of Scripture.

Moreover, the New Testament gives ample support to the unity of the prophecy in no less than twenty-one references which are made to it therein. It is this closing section which unites together the whole message of the prophet, whose theme has been that of condemnation, and who now brings to the people the theme of consolation.

You can never understand the ministry of any man unless you see it in relation to world conditions in which he lived. Since the death of King Hezekiah there had been a moral and spiritual decline in the land of Judah, which seemed to be incapable of any change. Apart from one, all rulers proved evil. Some years previously the northern kingdom of Israel had been taken captive by Assyria, and now Babylon had overcome the Assyrian empire. World power had changed again, and there seemed to be nothing to prevent the same fate overtaking the southern kingdom of Judah. Jeremiah, Isaiah, Micah, and other prophets, also Hezekiah the king, had all pleaded in vain with this people who had known so much of the blessing of God, but who now stood, at the very moment in which Isaiah preached, on the brink of apparent disaster and of the chastening, disciplining hand of God, as they were about to enter the captivity of Babylon. They were a people laden with sin, disobedient to the revelation of God's truth and His prophets; a people who, with every facility and every opportunity to repent and turn to Him, were now about to reap the inevitable consequence of disobedience. It was at this moment, poised at the very brink of a period of chastening and captivity, in which the message of Isaiah sounded out, "Comfort ye, comfort ye my people, saith your God" (Isaiah 40:1).

I cannot but wonder whether today messengers of God in the pulpits of our lands, prophets in evangelism and in other ways, stand to face a people poised at the very same moment in the history of the world, and especially that part known as the *free world*. Never in all history has civilization arrived at such a perilous, momentous period of time. Could it be that the chastening hand of God has come upon Western civilization as well as upon East Germany, China, and upon the church in many areas of the world? I do not know; but this much I do know, that Isaiah's message was not localized for his day, but is the dynamic, revolutionary, thrilling message for the day in which we live right now. I would remind you of the tremendous sweep of the message in this prophecy, as he stands confronting a people about to undergo the chastening hand of God.

Have you considered in the study of your Bible the area covered by this section of Isaiah's prophecy? This is not my main theme, but I want to point out that the prophecy of Isaiah has 66 chapters, the same number as the books of the Bible. The first two sections have 39, the same number as the books in the Old Testament; the last section of the prophecy has 27, the same number as the books in the New Testament. In the last section of the prophecy, from chapters 40 to 66, there are three main themes and divisions that run through it: in chapters 40 to 48, on the eve of captivity, is the promise of deliverance; from chapters 49 to 57 there is a revelation of the One who is coming to deliver, and the Deliverer Himself is portrayed to us. Finally, from chapters 58 to 66 is the picture of a delivered people, the kind of folk they are after they have passed through the refining fires of the chastening of God.

So we see in the first of these divisions the promise of deliverance, and the central verse is 44:8, "Is there a God beside me? yea, there is no God; I know not any." Idols have gone, therefore deliverance is sure.

In the second division as Isaiah portrays to us the Deliverer Himself, the central verse is 53:5, "But he was wounded for our transgressions, he was bruised for our iniquities: the chastisement of our peace was upon him; and with his stripes we are healed." The Deliverer, the Saviour, has come.

The last division tells of the people who have been delivered, and the central verse is 62:3, "Thou shalt also be a crown of glory in the hand of the Lord, and a royal diadem in the hand of thy God." What an amazing picture of the unity of message as God speaks to His people on the eve of captivity!

This is not only Isaiah's message for his day; it is God's message to your heart and mine in our day. Here is the tremendous sweep of it, and the subject of it outlined for us in chapter 40. There is a message of deliverance, a message of One who is coming to deliver, and as the result of having been delivered, there is a complete transformation in the character of the people of God: they become a "diadem in the hand of our God."

What then is the subject of this prophecy? What is God saying to a people who stand on the very verge of captivity? There is a voice which speaks, and it comes not with condemnation but as a wonderful message of consolation and comfort as He says, ". . . comfort ye my people, saith your God. Speak ye [not comfortably as the Authorized Version has it but to the heart of] . . . Jerusalem"—not to her mind or conscience only, but to her heart.

Now I believe that in this day in which we live it is the tremendous privilege and task of the minister of God's Word to do just that very thing, whatever the future may hold for us, which God alone knows. He is on the throne, and all is in His hand. We stand in a place of great peril and danger, but God has a message for His people today, and His voice speaks to us from this passage of Scripture.

His first word is one of *forgiveness:* "Speak [to the heart of] Jerusalem, and cry unto her that her warfare is accomplished, that her iniquity is pardoned; for she hath received of the Lord's hand double for all her sins" (v. 2).

I want to pause to reflect upon this rather startling verse: "she hath received of the Lord's hand double for all her sins." Does this mean that the Lord is being so severe with her that He has punished her twice over? Of course it doesn't! The Bible is an Eastern book, and the illustrations therefore are taken from the Eastern way of life.

In those times, if a man was hopelessly in debt and unable to make payment, it was the custom for his creditor to write out a statement of his indebtedness, which he would nail to the door of the debtor's house. All who passed that way would know that here was a man who was bankrupt and unable to meet his obligations. The extent of the debt was there for all to see, for it was written on the parchment. But if it should be that the debtor had a wealthy friend, or someone who would come to pay his debt for him, and assist him by meeting his obligations, he would then go to the creditor and say, "I am prepared to accept responsibility for this man's indebtedness, and pay you now fully, and will give you the money." So immediately the creditor would go to the house of the debtor and cancel the amount of the debt on the parchment by folding it over double and sealing it to the door. That man had received *double* for all his indebtedness.

In the hour of testing and terror, Isaiah is commissioned to say to Jerusalem, "she hath received of the Lord's hand double for all her sins." Immediately this great evangelical prophet introduces us to the cross of Calvary where the Lord Jesus Christ was made sin for us that we may never have sin imputed to us, for "God was in Christ, reconciling the world unto himself, not imputing their trespasses unto them" (2 Corinthians 5:19).

If I speak to someone in this momentous hour of history, and in your own personal life there is a guilt complex, a sense of the burden of sinfulness weighing heavily upon you, of personal bankruptcy and failure—and you know that apart from the grace of God you are through—then the message from Him to you is to tell you that you have received *double*, not for some, nor for a few, but for all your sins. To make this fact a reality in your experience, there must first be the humble confession of your own sinfulness and need to the Lord, and then the acceptance by you personally of what He accomplished for all on the cross.

This is the first word that came to a people on the verge of their captivity. Mark you, the natural consequences of sin would usually remain. The punishment has to be taken. A man reaps what he has sown. David was forgiven for the tragedy of the affair with Bathsheba, but the sword of the Lord in chastisement was never to be taken from his home and children. To his dying day he knew forgiveness and cleansing, he knew all the pardon of God, but he lived for the rest of his life to bear the consequences of his sinfulness.

A sinful nation, such as Israel and Judah, must reap the consequences of their disobedience; nothing can stop the captivity for seventy years, and nothing can prevent the chastening hand of God being upon them. But through all the years of their captivity thére came ringing into their hearts and conscience, "We have received pardon, we have received double for all our sins!"

Though the chastening hand of God was upon them—and it may often have been heavy—the prophet had said, "Speak ye . . . to Jerusalem, that her warfare is accomplished, [and] that her iniquity is pardoned." (Isaiah 40:2). There was coming a time when God's hand would be taken off, when the punishment would have suited the crime, when God would set them free and bring them back. His people would come to their senses, recognize the sinfulness of disobedience and idolatry, and turn in repentance to Him.

"Your iniquity is pardoned, your warfare is ended, therefore because you have received double for all your sin, speak this word of authority and comfort to My people."

This, then, is the first voice that comes to us down through the centuries from this passage of Scripture. To many a person in whose heart there is that sense of complete failure and bankruptcy, with a sense of breakdown and utter frustration and futility in their own lives, the word that comes with authority from the Lord is, "You have received double for all your sin." It may be you are a Christian who is suffering the chastening hand of God, and taking the natural consequences of some failure in your life from which there is no escape. To you I would bring this word of comfort, and say that your warfare is accomplished. He knows when to release the pressure. He knows when to stop the chastening.

The voice of forgiveness is immediately followed by the voice of *deliverance*.

The writers of all four of the gospels refer to Isaiah 40:3 as related to John the Baptist, the one who is to come to prepare a highway for our God.

Here is the word of deliverance: "Every valley shall be exalted, and every mountain and hill shall be made low: and the crooked shall be made straight, and the rough places plain: And the glory of the Lord shall be revealed . . ." (v. 4, 5).

Just think of the background against which the prophet is preaching: in a comparatively short time they were going into a period of captivity; they would lose the song and the joy they once had, for there would be no song by the waters of Babylon. There they were under the chastening hand of God and, furthermore, they were under the hand of an oppressor who seemed to be all-powerful and far too strong for them. The situation must have seemed totally and completely hopeless. But when God speaks to the heart a word of forgiveness, it is only the prelude to an experience of His deliverance.

Forgiveness is not the end of Christian experience; it is only the beginning. Our Saviour's name was called Jesus, not that He might save us *in* our sins, but save us *from* our sins. The way back from Babylon to Judah was covered by at least a thirty-day journey through desert, over mountains, down into valleys. The journey must have seemed absolutely impossible, but when God takes a hand and steps in to deliver, the message of the prophet is that every mountain and hill shall be made low, the crooked shall be made straight, and the rough places plain.

It could be that you, too, know something of the chastening hand of the Lord upon you, and are saying in your heart, "There are so many crooked places that I can never get them straightened out; so many mountains that I could never possibly get through; so many valleys before me that all seems so dark. This could never be the right way! There is too much of a tangle, too many complications, too many problems!"

God has been allowing you to go through His chastening because of past failure, and the result seems to be that everything is so complicated and bewildering. But when He steps in to deliver, every mountain is laid low, every crooked place is made plain, and all the rough places become smooth. The promise that echoed into the captivity of the people of Isaiah's day was that there would be a day when God would deliver with His mighty power, and would set them free.

Have you experienced His forgiving power and His delivering mercy?

Has God stepped in to straighten out the crooked, to smooth over the rough, to lay low the mountain, and to exalt the valley?

When God forgives, He does it in order that He might completely deliver.

However, the prophet did not leave the people there: he left them with *assurance.* "The grass withereth, the flower fadeth: but the word of our God shall stand for ever" (v. 8).

The situation seemed to be so impossible. Their prophets were slain, their cities were in ruins. There was no hope at all of any human victory or deliverance. It was then the Word of the Lord through His prophet came to them in their captivity calling them to remember that all flesh is as grass that withers, *but* the Word of God endures forever.

God is not dependent upon man or methods, and one word of all His good promise has never failed. The authority of His Word is that upon which you can rest your heart in absolute assurance and confidence, that He who forgives and delivers will never break His promise.

Forgiveness is followed by deliverance, and God's Word is exactly that to your heart. The promise of deliverance is always accompanied by one of assurance, the bedrock of Scripture. Then it is all followed necessarily by a word of *testimony:* "O Zion, that bringest good tidings, get thee up into the high mountain; O Jerusalem, that bringest good tidings, lift up thy voice with strength; lift it up, be not afraid; say unto the cities of Judah, Behold your God" (v. 9).

The thrust of this word to the hearts of God's people was not for them simply to listen to what God had to say, but to believe it, appropriate it, and make it personal. As a result they were to blaze it abroad, for there was a responsibility placed upon each one of them who had been delivered and forgiven, and who had the assurance of His promise to spread around the glad tidings.

There was to be no apology for the message. There was to be no concern about suiting it to popular opinion: they had to lift up their voice with strength, and not be afraid. They had to speak with conviction, assurance, authority, with no apology and no excuse, that their God is the great God of victory and deliverance, and His Word never fails.

So often many Christians today have lost confidence in our message, and I will tell you why. We have lost it partly—not mainly—because it seems to so many people that Christianity is fighting a losing battle, and we are just on the way out. Every other faith is experiencing revival except the Christian faith. Consider the rise of Oriental religious faiths in the West, the way in which the spread of heathen religions is taking place throughout the whole world, while Christianity seems to be apparently a losing force with no vitality. Therefore, we are a little ashamed and apologetic for our message. But this is not the main reason.

Our soft-pedaling the Word of God, our fear to spread it abroad is due so often to the fact that the message is not real and vital in our own lives. Have *you* heard His Word of forgiveness? Do *you* look up into His face today as a sinner but, bless God, a forgiven sinner? Do *you* know that you have received *double* for all your sins? There is no record in heaven of any sin anywhere: we live just as though it had never happened. Is that true of you? Then if it is true, has that message been accompanied in your life by a real, vital, thrilling, transforming experience of the delivering power of the Holy Ghost setting you free from the grip of sin? Union with the Lord Jesus Christ enables a man to be not just a forgiven sinner, but a victorious saint; not just a forgiven soul, but a man living in the reality or the experience of deliverance from indwelling sin.

I firmly believe that, apart from God's intervening grace, man is totally and completely corrupt in everything he is. But, further, I believe that Jesus Christ has come into my life, not to leave me a crawling, weak, sinful creature, but to make me holy by His blood. I am persuaded that the vast majority of Christian people live their lives forgiven but beaten. Examine your own testimony by that statement: a forgiven sinner, knowing all the answers, but with God nothing more than the patron of your systematic theology instead of Jesus Christ the very lifeblood of your soul. It may be very convenient to set up Jesus as your *patron saint*—you don't do it intentionally—but what a mighty miracle takes place in a man when Jesus Christ becomes his life! Instead of the thorn there comes up the fir tree, and instead of the principle of the life of sin there is the principle of the life of holiness.

Lift up your voice, speak to the people, don't be ashamed of your message, preach it! But you cannot preach it unless you live it and know it. That is why we go around so ashamed; that is why the church says so little; that is why we have no vital, vibrant, thrilling testimony, because we do not know Jesus Christ in reality as our indwelling life.

Of course, we know doctrine, we know the Bible (or we think we do), but we don't know *Him*. O that, in these days, we may begin to know Him! To know Christ as our life, the One who has come to transform us into His likeness, who has come to deliver us, His people, that one day we, too, might be a diadem in the hand of our God!

What are we to preach? Well, what does the Book say? ". . . say unto the cities of Judah, Behold your God! Behold, the Lord God will come . . ." (v. 9, 10).

Picture this message getting into the conquering country of Babylon to a people suffering from the chastening of God because of their sins, and they are told, "Look for your God, He is coming to deliver you!" Imagine them expectantly watching for some great warrior heading a mighty army, some dazzling spectacle that would thrill their hearts, and what do they see? "He shall feed his flock like a shepherd: he shall gather the lambs with his arm, and carry them in his bosom, and shall gently lead those that are with young" (v. 11). What a paradox is the gospel!

We believe that Jesus is coming as King of kings and Lord of lords, and before Him every knee shall bow and every tongue confess that He is Lord. The day is coming soon when this poor world that has tasted all the bitterness of chastening and suffering, will taste the blessedness of the glory of the reign of the Lord Jesus Christ.

Yet the message of the captive people was not only that, but it was to point to a weak, suffering Man upon a cross, to the blood that streamed from His hands and His side, to the crown of thorns upon His brow, and say, "Behold your God!"

Look at Him! There He is, crucified in weakness, raised up and declared to be the Son of God horizoned before the whole world by His resurrection from the dead! If you want to see God as you want to know Him, you will see Him and know Him at Calvary. Paul declared this paradox when He said, "though he was crucified through weakness, yet he liveth by the power of God" (2 Corinthians 13:4).

If in your life there is a desperate sense of failure in spite of all your professions of Christ and of faith and religion, there comes to you this word of forgiveness: "Comfort ye . . . [you have] received . . . double for all [your] sins" (Isaiah 40:1, 2)! You have received forgiveness. The Lord your God shall come, and every mountain shall be laid low, every valley exalted, the crooked places straight, and the rough places plain. He will do this for you if you will meet Him at Calvary today.

There is a word of deliverance because it is based upon the assurance of the Word of God, and therefore it fits you, so go out without shame or fear, and speak to the people, "Behold your God!"

If you have been soft-pedaling your Christianity and have played up the social instead of the spiritual, the entertainment instead of the dynamic, revolutionary power of the Holy Spirit, then get to the cross where you may behold your God, and see Him—the living, victorious, mighty, risen Son of God—who is able to save to the uttermost all that come unto God by Him.

2

Isaiah 40:13–31

Why Argue with God?

Why sayest thou, O Jacob, and speakest, O Israel, My way is hid from the Lord, and my judgment is passed over from my God? (Isaiah 40:27)

The human heart is capable of going to many different extremes in its attitudes toward God. The heart that is cynical and rebellious will live in complete defiance of God and in complete disregard of any possibility of punishment or judgment. That is one extreme; but the other is the heart that is discouraged, distressed, frustrated, often giving way to depression and fear. Such will begin to use the language of our text, and to complain and argue with God, because they imagine their case is beyond Him.

This was the attitude of God's people in Isaiah's time at this particular point in their experience. They were about to enter a time of captivity. They were about to face—and had already experienced—something of the chastening hand of God for their sin and disobedience, and were therefore about to reap the harvest which they had sown. Instead, however, of searching their hearts about it, they began to say, "Our way is hid from God." In other words, guidance is impossible. "Our judgment is passed over from our God"—our deliverance is quite beyond His power.

Strange how we all use the same language in such circumstances! There are many reasons why we do. Sometimes it is because of the overwhelming sense of sin which is unpardoned, and there comes into the life: distress of heart, a consciousness of guilt, and a deep sense that somehow life has entered into a darkness from which there seems to be no escape, and there is no release from the sense of shame and guilt.

Sometimes a realization of the corruption of the flesh makes us use the language of the Apostle Paul in Romans 7:22-24 where writing, of course, as a Christian he says: "I delight in the law of God after the inward man: But I see another law in my members, warring against the law of my mind, and bringing me into captivity to the law of sin which is in my members. O wretched man that I am!"

At times there comes to our lives that experience and revelation of inward corruption which makes us begin to despair of ourselves.

It may not only be this. Sometimes it is because of a long experience of affliction, maybe of body or of mind, from which there seems no relief or escape, as year after year it is endured, and there seems to be no end. Other times it may just be the monotony of life, possibly the loneliness of it—just the aloneness of human experience—when we feel nobody understands.

Yes, it may be through one or other of these experiences that you have been passing these days, and because of it you have begun to question God's goodness and to say, "My way is hid from God. He cannot guide me . . . My judgment is passed over from my God; He cannot deliver me. My case is beyond Him." In such an attitude of despair you may find yourself now.

What does God say to people facing this? I am so thankful that He condescends (and I think that is the right word) to say something. I am so glad that He speaks, and that He has an answer. So I want you to notice in the first place here in this very text, before we examine the context, that He reminded the people who were complaining who they really were: "Why sayest thou, O Jacob, and speakest, O Israel . . ." (Isaiah 40:27)?

God's first step to answer the complaint of His people was to remind them of their great covenant relationship which no power on earth could ever sever, and He says to this people who looked into His face in complaint and grumbling, "Do you remember what I said to Jacob when I first met him? 'I will not leave thee, until I have done that which I have spoken to thee of' (Genesis 28:15). You say I cannot guide you; you say your way is hid from me. I would remind you of the beginning of our relationship when I told you I would never leave the task half done, nor would I ever leave you until I had done all that I have spoken to you of. Do you remember a day when I changed your name from Jacob to Israel? I said to you then, 'Thy name shall be called no more Jacob, but Israel: for as a prince hast thou power with God . . . and hast prevailed' (Genesis 32:28). You say that your case is so hard and desperate that I cannot deliver you. I remind you there was a day when I spoke of an experience that would take place in your life, when I would change your name with the significance that I was going to change your character. Do you mean to tell Me that I have forgotten this?"

So to the one who begins to complain against God's ways instead of seeking in his own heart whether or not there may be a reason, God's first answer is to bring him right back to covenant relationship, to remind him of the pit from whence he is digged, of the fountain which washes away all sin, of a living Christ, omnipotent at the right hand of the Father, who is able to save to the very uttermost all who come unto God through Him, and to remind him that with God nothing shall be impossible.

To the life today burdened with a sense of unforgiven sin, or suffering from a revelation of a personal experience of the corruption of the flesh, to a person facing that sense of loneliness and misunderstanding and desolation in life, I remind you of the promises of God that are Yea and Amen in Jesus Christ. Therefore, if you are to find the answer as to why it is you complain with God, why affliction seems so persistent and loneliness seems to continue, why prayer seems to be unanswered, and there is such a sense of guilt and corruption, then you must look somewhere else than the character of God.

I notice from the context of this tremendous chapter that the Lord brings to these people a threefold answer that I, too,

would bring to some troubled soul today in Jesus' name, and I
trust that the message may ring with the same conviction as it
did through the lips of Isaiah.

In the first place will you notice He brought to them the
answer of *His omnipotence* (v. 12). I wonder if there has ever
been written such majestic language as this. Here is God an-
swering people with a burden of guilt, and a sense of oppression
and perhaps corruption, and what does He say to them? "Who
hath measured the waters in the hollow of his hand, and meted
out heaven with the span, and comprehended the dust of the
earth in a measure, and weighed the mountains in scales, and
the hills in a balance?"

Oh, the vastness of the reach of the hand of Almighty God!
As I read this verse I see myself being taken by the shore of the
ocean, and in my mind I conjure up all the oceans of the world,
and hear God saying to me that He measures them in the hollow
of His hand!

He makes me see the great mountain ranges of the Himalayas
and the Rockies, and He tells me that He can pick them up and
weigh them, just like the storekeeper who supplies our daily
groceries can weigh the goods in a scale! He is so omnipotent
that He can pick up mountains and weigh them as in a balance!

Oh the vastness of the reach of God, that can stretch right
around this globe that we call our earth, and hold the oceans in
the hollow of His hand, and the mountains in scales!

Then He speaks to us about the greatness of His wisdom
(v. 13, 14): "Who hath directed the Spirit of the Lord, or being
his counsellor hath taught him? With whom took he counsel,
and who instructed him, and taught him in the path of judgment, and taught him knowledge, and shewed to him the way
of understanding?"

He takes my little, miserable, complaining experience that
grumbles with Him, and holding me in His presence I hear Him
say, "Who do you think taught Me to make this great universe?
With whom do you think I conferred when I flung it all in space?
Whom do you think I sought guidance from then? Who instructed Me on that day when, in the counsels of eternity, I

created all this? for in the beginning God created the heaven and the earth."

Somehow my complaint seems to make me blush, and my grumbling makes me want to hide my face in confusion from a God like that.

Then He reminds me not only of the vastness of His reach and the greatness of His wisdom, but of the insignificance of the nations: "Behold, the nations are as a drop of a bucket, and are counted as the small dust of the balance: behold, he taketh up the isles as a very little thing" (v. 15).

The greatest of them, the most powerful and idolatrous of them, the most wicked and sinful of them, the most terrifying of them—all the nations are as a drop in a bucket, so insignificant in reality.

As I face a God like this, and then think also of my puny complaints, I hear Him say (v. 16), "If you took all the cedars of Lebanon, and all the cattle and every animal you could find, all would be totally inadequate to bring before such a God as an offering of praise and worship."

Oh the omnipotence of God, for the Lord God omnipotent reigneth!

Do you still say He cannot guide you? You say your situation is beyond His control, and that it is beyond Him to deliver. You say that the desolation and loneliness of life are too much to bear—"Why sayest thou, O Jacob, and speakest, O Israel . . .?" (v. 27). You say your way is hid from Him, and your judgment has been passed over, and yet He is your God!

But this does not answer your problem. If He is indeed your God—and somehow your soul and every part of you bows before Him in worship and acknowledges Him to be your Lord, the Omnipotent One—this still does not answer your problem.

"Why," you ask, "if this be so, do I experience no guidance? Why can I not see my way clear? Why does the Lord leave me alone? Why the misery, the defeat, the corruption? Why? Why?"

The answer of His omnipotence is followed by the answer of *His comparison:* "To whom then will ye liken God? or what likeness will ye compare unto him?" (v. 18).

Yes, these are His people, and He is holding them, as it were (and I trust He is holding you at this moment), before His gaze. His eyes are fixed upon them to challenge them: "To whom then will ye liken me, or what likeness will ye compare with me?"

Why does He ask that question? Because this people (as you know, from the record of Scripture) in times of sin and disobedience, when they experienced the chastening hand of God, instead of heart-searching and repentance, what did they do? They manufactured a god of their own, and "The workman melteth a graven image, and the goldsmith spreadeth it over with gold, and casteth silver chains" (v. 19). In other words, he made the best job he could of it. He made it shine, he polished it, and the result was nice and refined.

But some people were so poor they could not afford such luxuries, so they hacked down a tree which looked as if it would last a long time, and employed a cunning workman to prepare a graven image that would never be moved, something that would be permanent and lasting (v. 20). Thus they substituted impotence for deity, death for life, religion for the living God. So He begins to speak to them about this.

"You say," He says, "that I am not guiding you, and that you are not experiencing deliverance. Now before you question Me, let Me ask you something: what have you substituted in your heart for Me?"

Maybe we are not as crude as the ancient Israelites, though some nations are. However, some people worship a crucifix, others will worship the church, or idolize the preacher. Some people will bow before the gods of materialism, ambition, sex, even home and loved ones, and will substitute anything if only they can escape having to get down to the basic need of facing why it is that God does not guide or deliver.

I find in my heart that nothing is so costly for me as genuine repentance of sin. There is something very deep in my life that would rather face anything than that; and while I would not erect an image, or be so stupid as to build something and worship before it, how often you and I do something which is just as stubborn.

As we raise the question before heaven, "Lord, why is there no guidance? Why is my way hid from You? Lord, why is it there is no deliverance in my life?" God speaks straight to the depths of the soul, "Who or what have you put in place of Me? To whom then will you liken Me?"

As you read Isaiah's message, you notice how addicted the people were, how determined and devoted in their idol worship. They were determined, somehow or other, to build up their case, and to erect this heathen system of worship and idolatry rather than face the Omnipotent Lord with the fact of sin. Here is the answer of comparison.

Perhaps God is speaking to your heart in answer to your complaint with His way, and asking about the substitutes you have erected in your life.

What about the idols in your thought life?

What about the things that flood your imagination day and night, the secret desires that are unknown to all except to the Lord?

We have built up our system of religion, our churches, our theology. We have built up our lives and covered up under the fact that we can say, "Well, after all, I am preparing to be a missionary . . . After all, I have given Him my talents . . . After all, I am going to college . . . After all, I have dedicated my life to Jesus Christ . . . After all, I am doing this and that, and am proving before heaven and before men that I am a consecrated soul."

Stop! God doesn't want your cleverness; He wants your cleanness. That is something utterly impossible apart from the blood of Jesus Christ. It is remarkable how far a Christian can go in covering up along this line. He can gain a position in the ministry or in his church, or in Christian work, and be counted a great leader or teacher, but in the eyes of God he is a hypocrite, for

all the time he has built up in his soul a substitute for the risen
Lord.

God gave to His people the answer of His omnipotence and,
having asked them to think how it could ever be possible that
they could lose their way of deliverance in the face of that, then
He turns the arrow straight back into their own lives, and asks
them to face the comparison.

But God's last word (and how thankful I am, and I am sure
you are too) is never judgment, but deliverance. So God faces
His people with the amazing answer of *equality:* "Have ye not
known? have ye not heard? hath it not been told you from the
beginning? have ye not understood from the foundations of the
earth? . . . Yea, they shall not be planted; yea, they shall not be
sown: yea, their stock shall not take root in the earth: and he
shall also blow upon them, and they shall wither, and the whirlwind shall take them away as stubble" (v. 21, 24).

That is what happens to the gods that we have worshiped in
place of our living Lord. That is what happens when you get out
into the whirlwind of life and death, to find that every substitute
which is put there in place of Jehovah is an absolute sham.
When God strikes in the time of whirlwind, all is found to be
chaff.

But He asks again, "To whom then will ye liken me, or shall
I be equal? saith the Holy One. Lift up your eyes on high, and
behold who hath created these things, that bringeth out their
host by number: he calleth them all by names by the greatness
of his might, for that he is strong in power; not one faileth"
(v. 25, 26). "Hast thou not known? hast thou not heard, that the
everlasting God, the Lord, the Creator of the ends of the earth,
fainteth not, neither is weary? there is no searching of his understanding. He giveth power to the faint; and to them that
have no might he increaseth strength. Even the youths shall
faint and be weary, and the young men shall utterly fall"
(v. 28–30).

Wait a minute! There is some light here for my soul on this
matter of my complaining. Do you notice the contrast? The
everlasting God faints not, He is not weary; but I faint and

become weary, not merely physically or mentally, but spiritually. You and I know absolute exhaustion which brings upon our lips the unworthy argument with God. Yes, we become faint and weary and baffled. Then we cry out, "Lord, why is there no deliverance?"

But the everlasting God is not weary, and never faints.

Why do I faint and tire? Because of sin that has severed my connection between the One who is omnipotent and all-powerful. That is why.

Does this begin to throw light upon the problem of a seeming lack of guidance and deliverance? When we sever the connection between His omnipotence and try to fight it out in our own way and in our own strength, then we become utterly weary.

The Almighty One is not weary or faint. Can it be that He wants to make us like Him? Yes, He does, for ". . . they that wait upon the Lord shall renew their strength; they shall mount up with wings as eagles; they shall run, and not be weary; and they shall walk, and not faint" (v. 31).

Isn't the whole genius of redemption to turn sinful men into godly people? The whole theme of salvation is to stamp out the image of sin, and stamp in the image of Jesus, until He presents the church spotless before the Father, without flaw, His holy bride.

There is a strange order of events here: "They shall mount up with wings . . . they shall run . . . they shall walk." I learned to walk before I could run, and I learned to run before—well, I haven't learned to fly yet, though, of course, that is the ambition of the whole human race in its space travel! The church is going to indulge in some wonderful space travel when Jesus comes again: the moon will be bypassed en route to glory!

But isn't this a strange order? Walk, run, faint—NO! Walk, run, mount—NO! God says they shall first mount up with wings, then they will run, and then they will walk and never faint. That is heaven's order. Why?

They that wait upon the Lord shall mount up into heavenly places in Jesus Christ, and take their place where God has put them, with their hearts in heaven and their feet on the ground.

They shall know that they have been brought by Jesus Christ to a place of identification with Him in His risen life where they are far above every situation, every complaint, every circumstance, and every defeat. For in Jesus, and in Him alone, there is the path of guidance and deliverance.

They that wait upon the Lord begin by mounting up just there, and because they take the place where God has put them, they will run and never be weary, they will walk and never faint.

I do not find anything in my Bible about the fact that I am going to run in heaven, or that I will mount up with wings when I get to glory, but I do find a lot of walking. ". . . they shall walk with me in white" (Revelation 3:4), those who "have washed their robes, and made them white in the blood of the Lamb" (v. 14).

You may be one who is frustrated with a sense of loneliness and aloneness: "they shall walk *with Me.*"

How does renewal begin? "They that wait upon the Lord shall exchange their strength for His." What does it mean to wait upon God? I will tell you: it means silence, no more complaints, no arguing with Him. It means communion with Him in the secret place of prayer. It means the light of the knowledge of the glory of God shed in your hearts in the face of Jesus Christ.

That is the end of loneliness. It is the end also of overwhelming guilt, and of being baffled and beaten by inward corruption. From that moment onward He comes into you with His inexhaustible supply and with His strengthening life, and never again do you ever expect anything but corruption from the flesh, from all that is you apart from Jesus.

The ways of guidance and deliverance are right open, if you are prepared to stop arguing with God, to turn with all your heart to Him, for He has promised that if you do, you shall surely find Him.

3

Isaiah 41

God Is Still on the Throne

*Fear thou not; for I am with thee: be not dismayed; for I am
thy God: I will strengthen thee; yea, I will help thee; yea,
I will uphold thee with the right hand of my righteousness.*
(Isaiah 41:10)

This chapter is the great I WILL chapter of the Bible. No
fewer than fourteen times in the scope of these verses does God
reinforce His authority with this promise, "I will."

Let us take a brief look at them, to feast upon them and ask
that God may make them real to each of us personally. Notice
them carefully. There are three of them in verse 10: "I will
strengthen thee; . . . I will help thee; . . . I will uphold thee."

Verse 13: "I . . . will hold thy right hand . . . ; I will help thee."

Verse 14: ". . . I will help thee."

Verse 15: "I will make thee. . . ."

Verse 17: "I . . . will hear them, [and] . . . will not forsake
them."

Verse 18: "I will open rivers in high places, . . . I will make
the wilderness a pool of water. . . ."

Verse 19: "I will plant in the wilderness the cedar . . . ; I will
set in the desert the fir tree. . . ."

Verse 27: ". . . I will give to Jerusalem one that bringeth good
tidings."

When God says, "I will," He says it with all the authority of
omnipotence. He has foreseen every difficulty. He has studied

every obstacle which may come in His way. He has anticipated every possible contingency. He knows the weakness of the one to whom He makes His promise, and yet He says, "I will!"

No wonder, therefore, that three times in this chapter there is a further word emphasized: "Fear thou not . . ." (v. 10, 13); "Fear not, thou worm Jacob . . ." (v. 14).

Now if we are to get the significance of this tremendous chapter full of God's promises, we need to see it in its setting, which is most revealing and challenging. Think of the arena for the display of omnipotence.

Look as God creates, as it were, the platform upon which He is going to display His glory. In this chapter He is pictured as summoning the whole earth as far as the remotest islands to determine once and for all, and to settle the issue, who is the true God: whether he is like the idols which myriads of people have worshiped in every nation under heaven, or whether He is who He claims to be.

So you have this introduction in the first part of the chapter: "Keep silence before me, O islands; and let the people renew their strength: let them come near; then let them speak: let us come near together to judgment" (Isaiah 41:1).

Here is the Almighty God calling to the uttermost ends of the earth for a consultation to settle an issue finally, and the test that is proposed is very simple. The gods of heathen nations are invited to predict events in the future, or to show that they had any understanding of events of former days.

"Produce your cause, saith the Lord; bring forth your strong reasons, saith the King of Jacob. Let them bring them forth, and shew us what shall happen [in other words, predict the future if you can]: let them shew the former things [let them explain history], what they be, that we may consider them, and know the latter end of them; or declare us things for to come" (v. 21, 22).

Here is the challenge of One who claims to be omnipotent directed against all who claim to be worthy of the worship of another, and He says, "Very well, then. Come before Me!" Here is the court of appeal, and heaven invites everyone to come to it.

You notice that Jehovah demonstrates His ability to do the very things which He challenges other gods to do. As to the past, He has raised up one from the east whom He called in right-eousness. This is probably a reference to Abraham. He "called him to his foot . . . and made him rule over kings" (v. 2). As to the future, He would raise up one from the north who would deliver His people from captivity (v. 25). This is undoubtedly a reference to Cyrus, King of Persia.

Thus God demonstrated His ability to explain the past, to predict the future, and He is not afraid to face the whole world and challenge every idol to do the same.

Now the result of this challenge was a great commotion: "The isles saw it, and feared; the ends of the earth were afraid, drew near, and came" (v. 5). Fear struck the people as they drew near to judge their cause, and on the way—what a graphic picture this is in verse 7—as they were gathering to meet the challenge of omnipotence, they industriously polished up their dilapi-dated gods, and made new ones determined, of course, to put the best show upon their idol worship that they could! But when they faced Jehovah the idols were dumb: not one of them could speak. Not one of them had a word to say concerning the sub-ject submitted to them.

As the Lord looked upon them (v. 28, 29), He declared that there was no counselor who could answer a word: "Behold," He says, "they are all vanity; their works are nothing: their molten images are wind and confusion"—and the idols are silent. They have no answer to the challenge of omnipotence.

This is the platform not merely of Jewish history, but of con-temporary Christianity, upon which the church stands today in the midst of a tremendous battlefield. The spiritual conflict experienced today is exactly of the same nature and of the same character as you find depicted here. The issue is still unsettled in the minds of men, though it is settled eternally in the mind of God. The world is still making every effort to put the best possible show upon its worship of the creature rather than the Creator. Its worship is more the patronizing of the shell of religion than bowing in submission before an empty cross, an occupied throne, and the King of kings in glory.

The eternal conflict is well described in the language of Psalm 2:2–4: "The kings of the earth set themselves, and the rulers take counsel together, against the Lord, and against his anointed, saying, Let us break their bands asunder, and cast away their cords from us. He that sitteth in the heavens shall laugh: the Lord shall have them in derision."

The tremendous spiritual battle between Almighty God and those who would challenge His authority is rapidly coming to a climax in which He will demonstrate His authority once and for all, and the whole world will be on its face before the throne of God in acknowledgment that He is King of kings.

As this great warfare is engaging itself all around us with increasing intensity, in the midst of it there are little groups of people—and you will find them everywhere—who have been redeemed by the blood of the Lamb, who have been born of His nature, indwelt by His Spirit, who are marching onward to Zion —the people of God. God's interests today are not in Britain, in America, nor in the Soviet Union or in China. They are in His blood-bought people.

Paul, writing to the church at Ephesus, tells how God has declared and revealed to him a mystery which was hid with Him from the very foundation of the world—the mystery of the church and of the gospel, about which Paul was commissioned to preach. Why? In order that now, in this our day and generation, "to the principalities and powers in heavenly places might be known by the church the manifold wisdom of God" (Ephesians 3:10). In the second chapter of the same letter and the sixth verse he says, concerning God's people, that He "hath raised us up together, and made us sit together in heavenly places in Christ Jesus." Why? "That in the ages to come he might shew the exceeding riches of his grace in his kindness toward us through Christ Jesus" (v. 7).

God's interests are not in preserving a nation but in preserving His people. You might well panic at the state of world conditions until you realize that His purpose and plan for today is that He might make known in heavenly places, to principalities and powers, His manifold wisdom, and that He might do it through His blood-bought people. What condescension and what privilege! In all the ages to come throughout eternity He has caused, in the midst of a generation that has gone completely mad, His people to sit with Him in heavenly places, with their feet on the ground—in the very place where principalities and powers contest this battle with omnipotence. And all in order that there might be made known the riches of His grace according to His kindness to us in Jesus Christ.

Here, then, is the platform upon which God is to display in this day His glory to every idol, every heathen, every individual, and will reveal to them that He is, in fact, omnipotent, and His interests are in His people.

Well, if this be so, what do I expect to find concerning His people? They must be invested with a great deal of power to stand such days as these, and presumably we are going to find them in high and influential places. We would expect to find them in possession of great ability and talent, possibly possessed with quite an amount of worldly goods, men who are able to meet men on their intellectual level and answer back. In short, men of some prominence. Do I find God's people there? I do not.

Isaiah 41:17 describes them as poor and needy. They seek water and there is none. The heights are bare, and the valleys without pasture. Their journey takes them through a wilderness. They are as powerless as a weak, wriggly worm (v. 14)!

It is among people like this that God finds His own, not among the wise or prudent, but the babes; not among the high and mighty, but the lowly and obscure, the nobodys or people who are prepared to reckon themselves as such. This is how the Apostle Paul described Christians in 1 Corinthians 1:26–29, "ye see your calling, brethren, how that not many wise men after the flesh, not many mighty, not many noble, are called: But God hath chosen the foolish things of the world to confound the wise; and God hath chosen the weak things of the world to confound the things which are mighty; And base things of the world, and things which are despised, hath God chosen, yea, and things which are not, to bring to nought things that are: That no flesh should glory in his presence."

Now it is people like this in whom God is interested, and it is such people through whom He is working, who are to be the platform for the display of His glory.

Why should they be like this? I will tell you why: God needs room in which to work. Have you got that in your own heart? He needs empty vessels which He can fill. He needs weakness which He can empower in order that no flesh might glory in His presence. The lower and more humble the platform, the greater is the proof of what God can do and be to those who trust Him.

The greatest blessing of His kingdom, the arena upon which He displays His glory, is the man who is poor in spirit, persecuted, emptied, suffering and starving for God. To such a man He says, "Fear thou not; for I am with thee" (Isaiah 41:10). He comes nearer to him and says, "I will strengthen thee." Then He comes still nearer and says, "I will help thee"; until He puts His arm around him and says, "I will uphold thee with the right hand of my righteousness!"

Now the circumstances in which the glory of God is going to be displayed in His people are as varied as thought can make them. You could, in your imagination, go to a prison in Nepal where you would find a little group of believers being starved to death simply because they dared to make Christ known to others. They are our kith and kin in Christ. We have never met them; they are from a different background, a different color; but we shall meet them in glory.

You could go in your imagination to inland China and see horrors which are beyond description. You could go to South America, to Africa or the Soviet Union, and you will find every attempt being made to suffocate the child of God, to throttle the Christian church, and wipe it out of existence. It is such people as these with whom the Lord is concerned, and through whom He is displaying His power.

Now we may not be in these countries nor experiencing these situations and circumstances, but at the same time some may be going through such intense physical suffering that sleep and rest are impossible. You may feel you have suffered far more than is your due. Listen to the voice of your loving Lord as He speaks with all authority, "I am with thee." He knew what would happen; He foresaw and permitted it, for nothing has ever happened in the lives of His people but that it has first passed through His presence. The good Shepherd goes before His sheep, and tastes every experience before it touches them. "For our light affliction, which is but for a moment, worketh for us a far more exceeding and eternal weight of glory" (2 Corinthians 4:17).

Perhaps you have been through such sorrow that your heart is utterly broken, and the bottom has fallen out of your life. Maybe loved ones have been snatched from you—a little baby, or a lifelong partner or friend. The world has lost its song for some, but to such a one God comes and says, "Fear thou not; for I am with thee." He knows, He understands and maybe (I am not attempting to be an interpreter of Providence) He sometimes has to remove the earthly that He might make the heavenly more real. Sometimes He takes away that which is most precious so that into the void of a life that is utterly broken He may pour the glory of His indwelling love.

If such is your condition, you learn to say with Job, "Though he slay me, yet will I trust in him" (Job 13:15), remembering that the Captain of your salvation was made perfect through suffering. My heart goes out to such.

It could be you are faced with adverse circumstances: your business is falling apart; you are without employment. You find yourself being swept downstream with a family to maintain, and you have nothing to do it on. God says to you today, "Fear thou not; for I am with thee." Remember Him who for our sakes became poor that we, through His poverty, might be made rich.

In life He had nowhere to lay His head; in death a borrowed tomb was His. He says, "My God shall supply all your need" (Philippians 4:19). Can you trust Him for that?

It may be that you have been placed in a position of unusual responsibility, and the Lord Himself has called you to a task which you feel is far beyond you. Are you plunging into it, or are you afraid of it? You think perhaps you were not wise in undertaking it, but God says, "Fear thou not; for I am with thee . . . (Isaiah 41:10). Cast thy burden upon the Lord, and He shall sustain thee" (Psalms 55:22).

Or do you find yourself today in the midst of opposition? Perhaps you are only in Christian work today at the price of complete scorn on the part of your parents. Maybe you are the only one who is a child of God in your home and in your family, and you have taken all the scathing sarcasm of people you love, but who are so ungodly they will not listen to you, and today you are desperately lonely. God says to you, "If ye be reproached for the name of Christ, happy are ye; for the spirit of glory and of God resteth upon you" (1 Peter 4:14). "Fear not, I am with you!"

I could go on endlessly in all kinds of differing circumstances, but I am seeking to apply a principle. The life of faith is like a ladder up to heaven which twists and turns, and appears not to be fastened to anything. It seems to hang in the air, and you see no further than the step on which you are standing. The next step seems to go out into an abyss, into oblivion, yet when you take it you find yourself upon a rock. Occasionally the clouds part before you, and then you catch a glimpse of the King in His glory, so eagerly you pick yourself up and go on. When you look back you are amazed as you realize how God has led. His voice is always saying, "Forward! Onward! Upward!" Often you would give up in despair were it not that He says to you, "Fear not!" As you look ahead today everything appears like a vast mountain; but as you look behind every mountain has become a plain.

Yes, this is the platform upon which God displays His glory. This is the arena in which omnipotence challenges impotence.

The Lord in His love assures us of His nearness, "Fear thou not; for I am with thee." What is the meaning of His presence? In all the affliction of His people, He is with us in sympathy. He is afflicted. He still says—as once He said to the persecuting Pharisee Saul, who sought to bring the whole church into disaster—"Why persecutest thou me" (Acts 22:7)? We have not a High Priest who cannot be touched with the feeling of our infirmities, but He is with us, not only in sympathy, but also in identity.

If in the life of faith, along the pathway of our walk with God, there is a place where even one of His people could fall, His name would be dishonored.

Have you ever watched, as I have done occasionally and breathlessly, two men climbing up the side of a precipitous mountain? One is the guide and the other is the man who is on the climbing expedition, fastened to his guide by a rope that is unbreakable. What happens to the guide happens to the man, and what happens to the man happens to the guide.

So it is in the life of the child of God. Dare I say this? If I don't get to heaven, neither will the Holy Spirit within me. Isn't that absurd? He came to dwell in my heart when I was born again, and He lives within me saying, "I will be with you forever." One day He is going to take me to the very presence of the King of kings, ransomed, healed, restored, forgiven, satisfied to awake in the likeness of the King Himself. And until then, what happens to me happens to Him. What happens to Him happens to me. That is the reality of His presence.

He is with us not only in identity and in sympathy, but He is with us in transforming power. Read Isaiah 41:15: the Lord has been speaking to "thou worm Jacob," then He says, "I will make thee a new sharp threshing instrument having teeth." I don't know of any other than the Creator Himself who can take a weak worm and make it sharp with teeth! God can do that. If there is somebody who feels just about as weak and wobbly as a little worm, that is the kind of life through which God displays His glory when He recreates it, making it a sharp, decisive instrument.

The greatest thing of all in this message, it seems to me, which I must say is this: if this is the platform upon which God displays His ability and power, if His blood-bought people are those in whom He is really interested and about whom He is concerned, then what happens to them in the journey? Where is the miracle of His power revealed?

Will the lifetime of sickness end? Probably not.

Will the loneliness and desolation of life stop? No.

Will the poverty be finished, and will employment open up? Not necessarily.

Will there be any change in outward circumstances? Probably not.

Does it mean that all the circumstances will continue the same—sickness or poverty without end? Probably so.

But there will be one great difference, and everybody will see it. Principalities and powers in heavenly places will observe it and know our Saviour and Lord is omnipotent, and that His purpose has triumphed, because only He can do this. Let me tell you what happens.

When a man sees with his soul the truth of what I have been saying to you, there suddenly bursts out of the night of his experience a shout of praise, a song of rejoicing, music and melody in his soul. What has made the praise, and what has caused him to rejoice? Simply this: he has believed the promise of our text (v. 10): "Fear thou not; for I am with thee"—not intellectually, but with a total commitment which has enabled him to lie down upon it. He has discovered, for the first time in his life, that every shattering experience that has happened to him has been focused to this one objective: to bring him to the place where he lies down in God.

Faith is conscious that God is there, and faith knows that His presence is the answer and the complement of every need. So the little desert bush of his life begins to glow and burn with reality that He is in him. Faith recognizes that God has entered into a covenant with His Son, sealed by His precious blood, which can never be dissolved. His faithfulness and love are bound to finish the task in a man's life which He has begun.

Faith knows that behind the chastening, the suffering, and the trial, behind that restriction of circumstance, there is a great purpose. The great Refiner of hearts has a meaning in every degree of heat which He allows the furnace to have.

Faith will anticipate the moment when we shall know as we have been known, and we shall understand what now we cannot see, for we shall see the goal for which God has been striving.

More important still, faith knows and understands that other people are watching, as well as principalities and powers, and learning from this experience of the redeemed child of God. They are watching his reactions; they are learning lessons which nothing else can teach; and glory is being brought to God as men, angels, and demons see (in the language of verse 20), "the hand of the Lord hath done this, and the Holy One of Israel hath created it."

Christian, remember you have been made—in the words of the Apostle Paul—a spectacle to the world, a gazingstock of men. This is how God deals with His people for it is the display of His greatness and love. Yes, he makes us like this, and puts us through it all, but what seems to be a desert in the minds of the onlooker has become the garden of the Lord in the soul. Right there He says, "I will open rivers in high places, and fountains in the midst of the valleys: I will make the wilderness a pool of water, and the dry land springs of water. I will plant in the wilderness the cedar . . . and the myrtle. . . . I will set in the desert the fir tree, and the pine, and the box tree together: That they may see, and know . . . that the hand of the Lord hath done this" (v. 18–20).

So the world, and heaven, and hell, watches.

In the world today—which is absolutely on fire, and is bringing enormous pressures to bear upon the Christian church— God is on the throne, watching over His people. And the greatest demonstration of His omnipotence is that a song comes in the desert, fruitfulness comes in the wilderness, and every experience and circumstance can be flooded with the glory of His presence.

In closing this chapter, turn to Psalm 23:

The Lord is my shepherd; I shall not want.

He maketh me to lie down in green pastures: he leadeth me beside the still waters. [In other words, He is in front of me.]

. . . though I walk through the valley of the shadow of death, I will fear no evil: for thou art with me; thy rod and thy staff they comfort me. [In other words, He is alongside me.]

. . . Surely goodness and mercy shall follow me all the days of my life: and I will dwell in the house of the Lord for ever.

He is behind me, He is with me, He is leading—and, hard-pressed Christian, redeemed by the blood of the Lord Jesus, going through the fire and the battle of testing—He is surrounding you! Yes, you are surrounded absolutely by the God of your salvation!

"Fear thou not; for I am with thee: be not dismayed; for I am thy God: I will strengthen thee; yea, I will help thee; yea, I will uphold thee with the right hand of my righteousness" (Isaiah 41:10).

Is He your Saviour, your Shepherd, your Lord? If so, what a platform you become for the display of His power.

I trust that this word will have some impact upon the lives of Christian people to prevent them behaving like worldlings in days like these, entering into panic-stricken fear because of what is happening around them. I trust they will recognize that our God is upon the throne, and most of all, that His interests are in His people.

It is my prayer, too, that it may have its impact upon others who are not His people, and perhaps—like those idols—polish themselves up to make the best show of religion, and do all they can in their worship of the creature instead of the Creator. May you come to recognize that only our God and Saviour Jesus Christ is omnipotent, and He displays His power not necessarily by changing our circumstances or relieving our sufferings, but by displaying the glow and glory of His indwelling presence in the lives of His people who are able to say, "I am persuaded, that neither death, nor life, nor angels, nor principalities, nor powers, nor things present, nor things to come, Nor height, nor depth, nor any other creature, shall be able to separate us from the love of God, which is in Christ Jesus our Lord" (Romans 8:38, 39).

Wouldn't you love to be surrounded by the love of a God like that? That is my nuclear bomb shelter, the only shelter I need!

4

No Crisis in Heaven

*A bruised reed shall he not break, and the smoking flax
shall he not quench: he shall bring forth judgment unto
truth.* (Isaiah 42:3).

Let us identify these words in Matthew 12:14–21.

Then the Pharisees went out, and held a council against
him, how they might destroy him. But when Jesus knew
it, he withdrew himself from thence: and great multitudes followed him, and he healed them all; And
charged them that they should not make him known:
That it might be fulfilled which was spoken by Esaias
the prophet, saying, Behold my servant, whom I have
chosen; my beloved, in whom my soul is well pleased: I
will put my spirit upon him, and he shall shew judgment to the Gentiles. He shall not strive, nor cry; neither shall any men hear his voice in the streets. A
bruised reed shall he not break, and smoking flax shall
he not quench, till he send forth judgment unto victory.
And in his name shall the Gentiles trust.

We have no problem about identifying the One referred
to in Isaiah 42: it all centers around our blessed Lord, and
we will think about Him. We can take different viewpoints,
vistas, vantage grounds, whatever you might like to call

them, and see Him from different angles. For these verses are
so full of Him, the Servant of Jehovah.

First, see Him as the Servant in His majesty.

You recall that the previous chapter painted a vivid picture
of the conflict that goes on constantly, and is yet continuing
around us, between forces of righteousness and those of evil,
and it concluded with the statement of absolute helplessness of
men apart from God: "Behold, they are all vanity; their works
are nothing: their molten images are wind and confusion."

But now by contrast, "Behold my servant"! When all others
fail, that is the time to look up and behold the Lamb of God. The
darker things become, the more eagerly do we look up to see
His lovely face, and the brightening of the dawn of His coming.

The fourth verse of this chapter is very wonderful: "He shall
not fail nor be discouraged, till he have set judgment in the
earth: and the isles shall wait for his law." We do not know when
Jesus will come again. We know He will come, He has said so,
and in such an hour as most men look not for Him. On that day
He *will* come, for the Word of God assures us that He will not
rest until He has subdued all things unto Himself, and put down
all sin.

When you think about it a moment, it is overwhelming, because He has undertaken a task which is beyond anyone other
than an omnipotent God. To save one soul requires a miracle,
but to save myriads of men and women from hell, from sin and
judgment, requires a myriad of miracles. To redeem a world
like this from corruption, and set up a kingdom of truth and
righteousness—what a project! It becomes all the more stagger-
ing when we realize that Jesus has chosen to do this through
such poor instruments as we are. For He works to accomplish
and to establish His kingdom through the means of His blood-
bought people, who are often so worldly and so lethargic.

If a man sets out to do a job, he demands that he must have
good tools with which to work. If he is a writer, then he must
have a pen with which he can write properly, or a first-class
typewriter. But our God works through all the imperfection of
His people, and He is not discouraged. He will not fail, says this

Scripture. The disciple may sleep, but the Lord will travail over a lost soul and agonize in prayer. The disciple may turn in the thick of the fight and run away, but our Lord will stand firm, for He who made the heavens and this earth of ours one day laid aside His splendor and became veiled in a body like ours—and God can never fail.

Notice what the first verse of this chapter says about Him: "my servant, whom I uphold."

We are introduced for a moment, as it were, into the sacred counsels of the Godhead, and here the Father is saying of the Son, "My servant—behold Him, whom I uphold."

The picture is taken from an Eastern court, where a monarch is in a procession, and as he walks he leans upon a favorite courtier. This verse, in fact, could well be translated, "Behold my servant, upon whom I lean." It is an indication of a special favor and confidence. So we have the picture of God the Father leaning upon God the Son, counting upon Him and trusting Him to fulfill all His purposes.

Furthermore, this verse tells us that He is One upon whom the Spirit of God dwells in all fullness. Therefore, this God who is trusted, upheld, loved, and anointed in heaven, is One who cannot fail. He shall bring forth judgment to the isles, to the ends of the earth.

Sometimes as we look around we don't think things look much like it! We get discouraged, and it seems as if our cause is lost, but that is simply because we work differently from the way God works.

We are always in a hurry, whereas God is never in haste.

We are often so noisy, while He is quiet and still: "He shall not cry, nor lift up, nor cause His voice to be heard in the streets." And silently His kingdom comes as the Holy Spirit drops His life into a poor, defeated, lonely heart, and comes to quicken him and enlighten him in truth.

The Lord does not need any prestige or fanfare. He does not need any pomp or splendor, neither talent or special learning. He works in silence. It may not look like it, but God is working, and He is on the throne.

Even if we doubt these things, Jesus Christ has accomplished already the greatest victory of all in that He laid the foundation of His kingdom at Calvary, where He paid the price for our redemption when, persevering through all the contradiction of men against Himself, set His face like a flint and never turned aside until on the cross He cried, "It is finished" (John 19:30)! And as we look at Calvary we see no half-salvation, no incomplete work: it is complete, perfect, and effective for the sins of the whole world.

Today we can look up to Christ in the glory because we have seen Him in the agony of the cross and in the triumph of an empty tomb; therefore we have the assurance that He will not fail nor be discouraged until He has brought forth judgment. I see, therefore, in these verses something of the mystery of the Saviour, the great majesty of the Servant of God, who is working out His purposes.

There is also something else here which is tremendous: the Servant of Jehovah in His great mercy to His people. "A bruised reed shall he not break, and the smoking flax shall he not quench: he shall bring forth judgment unto truth" (Isaiah 42:3).

There is a primary meaning to these words which is not the one I wish to stress, but as it is the first given to them we must not miss it. Matthew 12:14–21 is the New Testament commentary upon this Old Testament passage. The Lord Jesus was being assaulted by the scribes and Pharisees, but He refused to enter into controversy with them. They were merely bruised reeds and smoking flax. Had He chosen to do so, He could have broken and quenched them, but He had not come to drive out sin by argument or force, but rather to expel it by putting truth and righteousness in its place.

"A bruised reed shall he not break, and smoking flax shall he not quench, till he send forth judgment unto victory" (v. 20).

In other words, when He does that one day, that will be the end of every bruised reed and every smoking flax, for the hypocrite, the Pharisee, the formalist, and all His other enemies will then be finished.

That is the primary meaning of these words, and from them

we might do well to learn that the greatest way to fight what is wrong is to display truth. There is no need to get pugnacious, or to become argumentative and controversial. If you see a crooked stick in front of you, there is no need to start demonstrating to other people just how crooked it is—they can see that! Place a straight one alongside it, and the straightness of the one rebukes the crookedness of the other. If you want to stand against sin, then live Christ; if you want to rebuke error, then live the truth. This is the lesson to be learned from the Lord's words.

There is, however, another meaning here. A bruised reed is something that has suffered an injury. It is not entirely broken or beyond repair, but it is bruised. A smoking flax is something that is almost, but not quite, dying out. There is a spark somewhere, for it is still smoking.

In the case of the smoking flax, something has happened to it which, if it continues and is allowed to continue, will burst into flames.

Now note something in Isaiah 42:4, "He shall not fail nor be discouraged. . . ." This phrase applies to our Lord. "He shall not fail" is the same as the word *smoking*. He shall not "be discouraged": the word *discouraged* is also translated *bruised.*

So here is the Servant of the Lord of whom it is written, "He shall not fail nor be discouraged, till he have set judgment in the earth," for there are no bruises about Him; He is no mere smoking flax. He is well able to do the task of redemption because He is free from all the weaknesses and failures of His people. He has no flaws or blemishes—He is perfection and majestic strength.

Therefore, when I think of this and turn again to this statement, "A bruised reed"—crushed, trodden down—alas, what bruises have come to your life and mine because of sin! But here is One who stands beside us. He has no bruise or weakness, and from His position of power and perfection He can tell us that there is no life so bruised that need be utterly broken, there are none so injured in life who cannot be healed, or so depraved that they cannot be transformed. There is no man so far from

God that the blood of the Lord Jesus Christ cannot bring him near. No individual anywhere has been so gripped by sin that he cannot be set free and wrenched clear; for the virus of any sin, no matter how deep, can be cleansed and cured through the blood of the Lord Jesus Christ.

A bruised reed He will not break, but by His grace and power, in love and mercy, He will restore, renew, and re-impower.

I wonder if I speak to a bruised reed. Let me tell you there is no one beyond the reach of the Saviour's love, no one beyond the reach of His pardon. He looks upon the tremendous bulk of the sin of the whole world, and because He is without bruises and is no mere smoking flax, but burns as a living flame, He is able to cast all that mountain of sin into the depths of the sea.

Perhaps the bruised reed speaks of some heart today, crushed by the consciousness of sin and failure, but the revelation of a nature which you possess which seems to have a skin like an onion, for every time you remove one layer there is another inside which is even more offensive than the last. How conscious we are of this evil nature! Far behind in our experience is the sense of complacency about our imagined goodness—that has all gone.

Maybe I speak to some tender heart in which there is a deep conviction of sin. Let me tell you that you can be healed today by His hand of love.

Have you ever watched an expert gardener after a storm going through his garden, and looking after the wounded spray of some lovely plant that has been hanging down, not broken, but bruised and crushed? How tenderly he replaces it and carefully ties it up!

Just so does Jesus deal with the contrite heart. Whenever He finds repentance, believe me, immediately there He is with His pardoning touch and restoring power. A bruised reed He will not break.

But maybe you feel you are more like a smoking flax, and this, He says, He will not quench. We call ourselves Christians, but if you are like me, sometimes you are desperately ashamed of how dimly your light burns. There is far more smoke than fire:

so little prayer, so little real testimony, so much depression and discouragement. But the Lord says He will not extinguish the smoking flax.

How do you think you make a smoking flax take fire and begin to burn? First it must have oil, then it must have fresh air, and finally all the charred bits of rubbish around it must be removed to set it free. So the Lord brings to the dimly-burning life of some child of His the oil of His Spirit, the air of His Word, and by the discipline of His love—perhaps through sorrow or trial —He will take away the charred embers until that life begins to leap into a flame again.

Why is the flax of your life and of mine so dim? I will tell you: it is because we keep away from Jesus. He said in John 15:4, "Abide in me, and I in you. As the branch cannot bear fruit of itself, except it abide in the vine; no more can ye, except ye abide in me." Renew fellowship and obedience to the Lord, and the smoking flax of a slack Christian life will be revitalized into a flame for God.

So I see here the Servant of the Lord, not only in His majesty, but also in His mercy. I hope this warms your heart as it does mine.

Now observe Him in His ministry.

Look especially at these verses in this light. When our Lord took upon Him the form of a servant and one day took a towel, girded Himself, and washed the feet of His disciples (John 13:4, 5), it was not anything new that He was doing. If you think about it, the whole life of God (if I may say this reverently) is one of ministry. He is God because He serves. He governs and is omnipotent because He ministers. The life of Jesus Christ all along was a ministry, an exhibition and revelation of the life of God throughout all eternity.

Oh, that His Spirit would catch and wing this into our hearts until we begin to understand some of the principles upon which our service alone is acceptable to Him! For here is a model and example for all service. He wants to live in you and to repeat these principles of ministry in your life, that He might endue you with His Holy Spirit.

Think for a moment about the modesty of God. He is always at work: He guides the sun, the stars, and the universe. He controls every galaxy. He refreshes the earth constantly. But He works so quietly that many people now try to make out there is no God at all.

It was exactly like that with the Lord Jesus. He silenced the people who would proclaim His deity. Choosing privacy, He often stole away from the crowd, if you remember. He fulfilled completely the second verse of Isaiah 42: "He shall not cry, nor lift up, nor cause his voice to be heard in the street."

That is the hallmark of reality in service. God's artists do not put their signatures to the pictures they create. His ambassadors do not run after the photographer all the time to get their pictures taken. It is enough that they have borne witness to the Lord.

To win a soul for Jesus, to cleanse some scarred life, to help some bruised reed or smoking flax back into blessing, to look up from the task sometimes and catch a little smile from heaven, and to receive the reward of the Father who sees in secret—that is enough. Indeed, it is heaven beside which the praise or blame of other people is utterly valueless.

Is this the quality of your service, or do you seek the praise of other people? Do you want the press report, or magazine articles telling stories of your heroism? Be sure of this, if that is true, deterioration in your life is rapidly setting in. Withdraw yourself some time today in the presence of God, because you see, the only work which He approves is that which needs no advertisement. The bird in your garden is happy to sing, the flower is happy just to be lovely, that little baby in your home is happy to grow, and the true servant of God is just happy to do the will of God regardless of anything else.

As we consider the modesty of God, may we be forgiven our pride and our display!

Let us look deeper to see the humility of God. The Lord Jesus has always selected His disciples from among those who, in the eyes of the world, are very ordinary, and He reveals, He says,

His choicest secrets to those who are babes. He delights to
expend Himself on bruised reeds and smoking flax.

Think again of that reed: something that has been crushed,
or hurt by unkindness, a life that is somehow bent and bruised
and shattered, without strength or beauty. There is nothing
attractive about a reed, and there is certainly nothing very
pleasant about the circumstances in which it lives! Unusually it
grows in a smelly, unsavory swamp.

So it is that hearts get broken in the mad rush of this world,
by selfishness and cruelty and unkindness. You know, a heart
breaks very quietly. No one sees it happen except the Lord, and
He sees the day when, amid all the crush and impatience, the
fever-heat of modern living with its heartlessness and unkindness—suddenly a heart breaks. Nobody else notices, for in the
eyes of the world such a person is cast aside and regarded as
useless, devoid of attraction or beauty.

A smoking flax is so feeble that others scarcely believe there
is any love to God in it at all. Nobody would credit that there
was any evidence at all of life, but if this is a picture of you, *you*
know. Perhaps your other Christian friends misjudge you, for
you know the battle that goes on in your heart.

The superficial Christian worker ignores that kind of situation. He wants a sphere to serve where it will be worthy of his
talent, if you please. A task where his abilities will be recognized
and used, something that is big enough to justify all the training
he has undergone.

In the eyes of the Lord the test of the real servant is, does he
bend with the humility of Jesus Christ over a bruised reed and
smoking flax?

Are you ambitious for greater things in the Lord's work? Do
you grudge the trouble of taking time to talk to one poor soul,
to cope with the constant backsliding of the weak? Do you get
put out and irritated when you have to adjust your Christian
service to the constant quarreling of the weakest of God's children? Do you get frustrated when you have to set your pace to
the slowest of the learners? Then let me say to you, beware lest

the tenderness of Jesus is going away and fading from your life. Beware lest the grace of those early days is departing and decaying. Get alone with God and learn that the noblest soul in the sight of heaven is found among bruised reeds and smoking flax. Consider the humility of the risen Lord Jesus, and remember that He said that the servant was not above his Master.

Then, in conclusion, think of the perseverance of the Saviour. "He shall not fail nor be discouraged": He has never slackened His hand, and He never will.

That which has its origin in the flesh is full of fury and hate, full of passion and zeal, full of impulse and emotion. It is often so hot, but it grows cold and gives up. The energy of the flesh peters out and balks when the going is hard.

It is the meek man who never turns aside from the purpose of God. Show me a man who will make up his mind about something, set to work, and patiently take all the rebuffs and knocks, the criticism and unkindness, and that man will never give in. He will finish that which he began because he possesses the grace of perseverance.

But the passionate and the easily excited will soon cool down because there is no depth of stability in their character.

You see, the Servant of Jehovah shall not cry, nor lift up, nor cause His voice to be heard in the street. He is quiet because He is sure. He is patient because He is strong. He is gentle because He is firm.

The man who cannot be provoked is the man whom you can never turn aside. Perseverance in the face of scorn, criticism, hatred, misunderstanding, rebuke, is proof that the task originated in heaven, and that the man of God is feeding on the resources of heaven in order to enable him to persevere.

That is the quality of Christian service that God looks for, and the secret is in verse 1: "I have put my spirit upon him." Ah, yes, in the power of that Spirit Jesus finished the task, offered Himself without spot through the eternal Spirit unto God. That anointing is for you and for me to be received by faith, to equip us for His work, and to enable us to persevere that we may be steadfast, unmoveable, always abounding in the work of the

Lord. God grant that we may be satisfied with nothing less. Indeed, perhaps we are, and maybe we need talking to by the Lord about it here and now.

Here are the principles of the Servant of Jehovah: modesty, humility, perseverance. Are these the driving forces in your life and service? Then I say, when they are, something happens in your heart and in your ministry: as you speak, His Spirit falls upon those who hear. As you witness to the glory of the Lord Jesus, the Holy Spirit witnesses to the heart and conscience of those who listen. When God's Word comes through your lips, the Holy Spirit says Amen, and in the heart of the people there is a responsive Amen. They may not always be in agreement, often not; but when the people have heard the testimony of one upon whose life there rests the anointing of the Spirit, they cannot remain indifferent.

How desperately you and I need that today, that He might say to us, "Behold my servant, . . . mine elect, in whom my soul delighteth"!

So I ask you to behold Him in His majesty, and may that give you confidence day by day.

Behold Him in His mercy, and may that give you comfort, and encourage some bruised and beaten heart.

Behold Him in His ministry, and may you have the confirming of His Holy Spirit as the principles of modesty, humility, and perseverance are yours by the appropriation of His saving and indwelling life.

5

Triumphant in Trouble

But now thus saith the Lord that created thee, O Jacob, and he that formed thee, O Israel, Fear not: for I have redeemed thee, I have called thee by thy name; thou art mine. When thou passest through the waters, I will be with thee; and through the rivers, they shall not overflow thee: when thou walkest through the fire, thou shalt not be burned; neither shall the flame kindle upon thee. For I am the Lord thy God, the Holy One of Israel, thy Saviour: I gave Egypt for thy ransom, Ethiopia and Seba for thee. (Isaiah 43:1–3).

Of course these words are primarily spoken to the Jewish people and, as you think about them in that context, how wonderfully they have been fulfilled through history. The story of the Jews is one of the great miracles of all time. In the world's history as they have faced one trial after another, passed through fire and water, been butchered and massacred, hunted, torn and scattered, they still live and thrive, because God has a great purpose for His own people, the Jews.

Had it not been that they were ordained to remain as His witnesses until their Messiah comes again, undoubtedly they must have perished, but they will continue to live until, as the Scripture says, they shall receive a new heart and a right spirit. Then the Lord will take away the blindness that has happened in part to Israel (as we read in Romans chapter 10), and they shall look on Him whom they have pierced, and mourn for Him

61

as one mourneth for his sons. On that day, the glory that was once theirs will be nothing compared to the glory yet to be.

Every promise in the Book, however, that is made to the actual people of God, the Jews, the seed after the flesh, is also made to the spiritual seed of which, according to Paul in Galatians 3:29, every believer in Christ is a part. Abraham was the father of all the faithful, and all believers are his seed, and therefore the father of all who trust in the living God. The church as a whole, throughout all history, will have this promise equally fulfilled to her. Indeed, already this has been proved so. How often the people of God have been through fire and water, but the floods have never drowned the church, nor the flames consumed her. No weapon that is formed against God's people can ever prosper. We who believe on the Lord Jesus, though it may not always appear so, are on the winning side—the side which has God and Christ and eternity with it. One day the heavenly Bridegroom will appear, and His bride will share His glory with Him.

Yes, this promise applies to the whole church, but more important for us at this time, it is spoken from God's heart to all who worship Him in spirit and truth. It is, as it were, as a personal word from His pen to us by His Spirit. This is how I desire we would receive it from Him. Therefore, as we look into these verses and apply them to our own lives personally, there are some very precious thoughts that come to us from this passage. Some of them, at first glance, may not appear to be precious, but they are when we understand them.

In the first place, it is quite clear that trouble is to be expected by the Christian. Some people seem to imagine that the man who is the object of God's special care and favor will never be tried, or have to suffer, but that is not true. Verse 1 tells us to fear not, for He has redeemed us and called us by our name. This is a very precious thing that God knows your name and mine, and calls us by it, and we are His.

Should we not conclude therefore that we should live at ease, and enjoy our blessings, and count them one by one? Should we not enjoy our luxuries and as His chosen people be protected from every possible harm? No. God's Word tells us that the man who is the heir of His kingdom is also the heir of tribulation, for Jesus said, "In the world you shall have tribulation; but be of good cheer, I have overcome the world" (John 16:33). If you and I are soldiers in His army, we do not win the victory without a conflct. If we are ordained to wear a crown, we are ordained to carry a cross, for the grace of God does not mean luxury, nor does it carry us to the skies on flowery beds of ease. If we would reign, then we must fight. If we would be glorified with Him, then we must suffer first.

Our text speaks of this as if it were taken for granted. It does not say, *If* thou passest through the waters, or *if* thou walkest through the fire; it says *when*. It is taken for granted that this is to be the experience of the people of God. Quite clearly we are told from this passage of Scripture that the troubles of God's people are very varied.

Conversationally, we often speak of "going through fire and water" as a way of describing a multitude of things that happen. The true child of God will have to go through the water—the kind of trial that chills him, that can sweep him off his feet, and carry him along in the current until somehow he feels he has lost control.

Then, when he has been through one trouble, another comes along over the horizon, perhaps a different kind, and instead of water it will be fire. From being chilled to the marrow, this time he is almost roasted in the furnace of affliction! It is one or the other.

When we lived in Chicago I heard of its reputation for weather, and it certainly lived up to it! How often in one day we had snow and rain, sunshine and wind, thunder and ice, and all the rest that heaven can send down within the space of a few hours. That was one of the charms of the city, you never knew what was coming next!

Now Christian experience is just like that: you never know what is coming next. The language of Isaiah 43 suggests that some of these things that come are going to be very severe. Let the language of this grip your heart (v. 2): "When thou passest

... through the rivers"—strong and mighty rivers, great powerful floods that bring damage and ruin, rivers that are uncross-
able. Yes, there are trials like these when it seems as if you can
never get through, and, alas, one time or another you become
convinced that your career as a Christian is finished, a complete
failure.

But what about the fire? If the floods overwhelm us, then the
fire will consume us. Yes, there is plenty going to happen between here and heaven to every child of God to destroy us
absolutely, unless we say with the Psalmist, "If it had not been
the Lord who was on our side, when men rose up against us:
Then they had swallowed us up quick, when their wrath was
kindled against us: Then the waters had overwhelmed us, the
stream had gone over our soul" (Psalm 124: 2–4).

I think, too, that this verse not only prophesies severe trials,
but it prophesies frequent ones. Look at the language of verse
2 again: first of all, water; then rivers; then fire; and as if that
is not enough, flame. Such is the lot of the people of God: water,
rivers, fire, flame.

Oh, yes, none of us have finished with temptation yet. Even
that which you thought you had overcome and left behind has
not finished with you. Nor have you yet tasted the limit of your
corruption, nor have you experienced the last of what Satan, the
world, and the flesh can do to you. It is not one fire, but many.
It is not one river, but many. And the hardest thing to take is
the constant, frequent repetition of one bitter experience after
another.

We are reminded of Job who first lost his servants, then his
sheep and the shepherds, then his family, and finally his health.
Blow upon blow, sorrow after sorrow, trouble after trouble—
such was this man's experience.

A soldier does not remove his uniform and lay down his gun
after one battle and say, "I have won the victory!" He is told that
it is but the beginning of a long campaign.

Further I would say that trouble is inevitable. Look at the
language again, "When thou passest through the waters. . . ."
It is taken for granted that you have to go through. There is no

bridge that you can walk over, no boat to take you across comfortably, no tunnel that undermines the trouble so you can get underneath it.

When the Lord speaks to us about passing through the fire, nothing is said about putting it out, or waiting until it cools off a bit. No, there is no suggestion that I wait until the flame has died down! I cannot expect merely to get my feet in trouble; I am called to pass through it. I do not just singe myself in the fire; I am called to go through the flame.

Sometimes, as Nebuchadnezzar commanded, it is heated seven times hotter, and the Christian who is living in the will of God goes through that. This is the appointed lot of God's people, and everyone of us will have more or less of this medicine. If you have more, then you will be given more grace. If you have less, be thankful for God's tenderness, and don't ask for more. But rest assured that all His children in their journey to heaven are going to have to face the fiery baptism of trial.

You may have what view you desire regarding the tribulation, as far as I am concerned, but some of our brethren in China, Korea, Eastern Europe could not go through worse than they are experiencing today.

God has had one Son without sin, but He has never had one child without suffering, never. All the sons and daughters of God are made to feel the chastening of a wise, loving, heavenly Father.

Here then is the first thing that comes to us from our text, that trouble is an essential part of the experience of the people of God.

The second lesson I see is that trouble does not destroy the people of God. Look at the first part of the second verse of the chapter: "When thou passest through the waters, I will be with thee." In other words, the waters, the trials and troubles, can never roll between me and my Saviour. The waters can never come between us, they can never divide or separate us from the living God.

Recall the language of the Apostle Paul (Romans 8:35, 38) in which the challenging question is asked: "Who shall separate us from the love of Christ?" And the answer comes with tremendous conviction, "I am persuaded, that neither death, nor life, nor angels, nor principalities, nor powers, nor things present [that is, the things which I am facing right now], nor things to come [that is, what may happen to me in the future], Nor height, nor depth, nor any other creature, shall be able to separate us from the love of God. . . ."

As I stop to think of that, I feel like running into any trouble, that I might prove the reality of Jesus Christ right there with me at the time! No flame matters if I am sure that it can never separate me from Him. If you are facing some of these things right now, you do not have less of Jesus because you might be sick or bedridden. Those people who claim to believe that the healing of the body is included in the atonement would do well to ponder on this, and to recognize that all that happens to the human body is part of the preciousness of the purpose of God for His redeemed child, that one day He might present him faultless in His presence.

Your losses and your crosses you will find are places where you realize the presence of Jesus as you never could have done without them. I do not find any promise in the Bible worded like this: "When you lie on soft green grass, or walk on a velvet carpet, I will be with thee." No, it says, "When thou passest through the waters, I will be with thee" (Isaiah 43:2), and just to meet our doubt, the Lord says, "I have redeemed thee, I have called thee by name; thou art mine" (v. 1).

Another thing I want you to notice is that it is quite clear that the water and fire do not stop the march of the people of God. We do not read: When thou gettest to the waters, thou shalt stop there! It says, "When thou passest through the waters. . . ." They cannot stop us: we go right through.

If our way to glory leads through the flood, then through the flood we will go. If our way to heaven leads us through the fire, through the fire we will pass. Nothing will ever stop the onward march of a soul of whom the Lord says, "whom he did foreknow, he also did predestinate to be conformed to the image of his Son, that he might be the firstborn among many brethren.

Moreover whom he did predestinate, them he also called: and whom he called, them he also justified: and whom he justified, them he also glorified" (Romans 8:29,30).

What a wonderful past tense is that experience—called, justified, glorified! In the mind of God we are in heaven now as though we were already taken there. Yes, He has begun, and He will never cease to perform.

Somebody says, "Oh, that is all very well, but I am not fireproof!"

But you will pass through the fire just as you passed through the water. Indeed the wonderful thing to me about this text is that it suggests that the march of a child of God through water and fire is so quiet, so calm, so safe.

What does it say? ". . . when thou walkest. . . ." It does not say, "When you run, or make a dash for it." In other words, in the very thick of the battle, when Satan is flinging everything at us, and we are going through the fire in one way or another, that is the time for the Christian to prove that he doesn't need to panic. There is no need for worry or haste—he just needs to walk. Of course, if it was literal fire, you would make a dash for it, you would be jet-propelled! But we are to walk spiritually.

"Though I walk through the valley of the shadow of death, I will fear no evil: for thou art with me," wrote King David.

Walking is the pace at which you go when you are not in a hurry, when you are not concerned or alarmed. When you are not burdened or anxious, then you walk. "He that believeth shall not make haste" (Isaiah 29:16). What a blessing!

So we are told from this word that no trouble can ever separate us from the Saviour. No trouble can ever hinder our progress toward heaven, and by His grace He will take us right through every obstacle. Mind you, we will often be out of our depth. Oh yes, in the deep experiences of life, the swimming of faith has made us cast everything we have and all we are upon the living God. Sometimes the waters will get near our heads, and dash in our faces; but they will not overflow or overwhelm us.

Sometimes the furnace may seem so intolerably hot that you

look up at God in the midst of it and say, "Lord, I just cannot take any more of it!" But you will come out of it as you went in—well, not quite.

You remember Daniel's friends who were flung by Nebuchadnezzar into a burning, fiery furnace, heated seven times hotter. To his amazement they stood, alive and unharmed, and he exclaimed in consternation, "Did we not cast three men bound? . . . I see four men loose, and [one is] like the Son of God" (Daniel 3:24, 25). The only thing they lost in the fire was the rope which bound them! They were loosened with not even the smell of fire upon them, and completely free!

It is a great thing when God sets you free. The gold loses nothing in the fire except that which is to be lost; the silver never loses any of its preciousness in the crucible, except the alloy.

> When through fiery trials thy pathway shall lie,
> My grace all-sufficient shall be thy supply;
> The flames shall not hurt thee, I only design
> Thy dross to consume, and thy gold to refine.
>
> GEORGE KEITH

So Hallelujah anyway! Yes, trouble is inevitable, inescapable, but in the midst of it, it is never something that destroys, but something which refines and purifies.

I am thinking now of a brother in the ministry whom I got to know during my years in Chicago. He was always smiling, such a happy radiant man, and just to look at his face was a blessing to me. I began to think to myself, "Of course, he doesn't know what it is to go through what I have to bear. He hasn't any of the burdens I have." You know the sort of thinking, full of self-pity, that deadly thing! I thought he had just a little church somewhere in the country with a few people, and I imagined life was easy for him—but how wrong I was! One day we had a banquet at Moody Church in connection with Mid-America Keswick at which there were about 250 people, ministers, Christian leaders, and their wives. To my amazement into the room came this dear brother in the Lord, carrying his wife who for seven years had been a cripple with polio. Ten years previously they had been missionaries, and now were ministering the Word at home. And they were both just radiant!

As I looked at that dear couple, how rebuked I felt in my own heart. There were no complaints, no questioning, but a sweetness and graciousness about them. It happened in a flash one day, when that lady was active in the Lord's service, and in five minutes' time she was on her back, never to walk again. She types letters by using a stick in her mouth, and maintains a sweet spirit of submission to the Lord's leading in her life. I know she would allow me to give this testimony to the glory of God.

I tell you this to show that when God puts a man through the fire and the flame, it may not always be physical. It may be spiritual. It may be an intense battle with the enemy of souls that seems relentless. It may be that all hell seems to be let loose upon you one way and another but, believe me, if a man is going to be matured and made like Jesus, then God puts him through it. May I lovingly say that if this is strange language to you, I would ask you to examine yourself whether you be in the faith at all?

My last word to you is to point out that tribulation discovers arguments for faith, and here are three of them. In Isaiah 43:3: "I am the Lord thy God." If our trust is in anyone or anything less than the Lord, then surely the flood will overwhelm, and the flame will destroy. But if we have a living faith that rests upon a living God, we shall never be confounded. No man who trusts in Him has ever been forsaken. If we rely on friends or human props, or even the church, all will fail; but the Lord cannot fail.

"I am the Lord *thy* God"—notice that word. Friends, be sure of that. He is yours because He has redeemed and sealed you; yours because He indwells you by His Spirit and possesses you. "the Lord thy God"—can each of us say that without question?

The second foundation for faith is also in verse 3: "the Holy One of Israel." When David said in Psalm 103, "Bless the Lord,

O my soul: and all that is within me, bless his holy name," why did he speak of His holiness before anything else? When God speaks of holiness He means wholeness. He cannot lie. A holy God cannot break a promise, and He guarantees to preserve His people Israel—and, in fact, all His people in every situation.

Yes, He is "the Holy One of Israel, thy Saviour." If He is to be true to that name, He must save all who put their trust in Him. "Many are the afflictions of the righteous: but the Lord delivereth him out of them all" (Psalm 34:19).

Thirdly, in the same verse, we read, "I gave Egypt for thy ransom, Ethiopia and Seba for thee" (Isaiah 43:3). In other words, the Lord says, "I have bought you at such a price that I cannot afford to lose you. The Israelites were redeemed as the Egyptians were made to suffer, and later Ethiopia and Seba were conquered by the Assyrian armies who turned upon them instead of turning upon Israel. God is prepared (and has already done so in history) to blot out nations for the sake of the redemption of His people.

I would remind you that He has paid a far higher price for us, something infinitely more precious than Egypt with all its treasure, or Ethiopia with its gold, or Seba with its fragrance. He has given His own lifeblood as a ransom at Calvary, and He cannot allow anyone whose faith and commitment are in Him to be cast into hell.

Jesus prayed in John 17:9, "I pray for them: I pray not for the world, but for them whom thou hast given me. . . ." It is absolutely inconceivable that a soul who has been given to the Son of God by the Father should ever fail to come into His presence, redeemed by His blood. Whatever could enslave a soul who has been set free? Yes, there are arguments here for our faith in which we may rest.

Many of you have proved through the years every word of what I have written. You have been through fire and water, and you bear the scars of conflict. But you never had a burden that was too heavy to carry, had you? You can say concerning your God that He has never failed. Yet is it not shameful that in spite of this we doubt Him. We say there are changing circumstances, we are getting old and shaky, and so on—but God never changes.

You have not passed through this particular circumstance before, no; but each one you have experienced has been new when you came to it the first time. It is not how you begin the Christian life that counts, but how you end it, that it might be said of you that you have fought a good fight, finished the course, and kept the faith.

But there may be some who do not know this God, and I really do not know how they exist. With no God to trust in, and unhappy circumstances, life is scarcely worth living, with its cares and worries. You are up early and go to bed late in order to try and earn some necessary cash, but what is it all for? Who will possess it one day when you die?

"But," you say, "we must have our fun!"

What fun? Dogs have their biscuits; cats have their food; hogs have their wash, and the world has its fun! When I see what some people say they enjoy I am almost tempted to wonder if they were absent when brains were being distributed! Ah, but let me be careful not to be sarcastic as, alas, there was a day when I myself was overwhelmed with it all. At least I can say that there is nothing to satisfy, nothing to last, nothing on which to feed the heart or the soul. There is no rest or peace or enjoyment for anyone out of the Lord Jesus.

How I pray that the word may drive you to find rest in the Lord, that your heart may find peace, that your burden may be lifted and your life cleansed in His blood. Then you, too, will learn to triumph in trouble, and you will find that as you are called to pass through the waters He will be with you. As you go through the rivers, they will not overflow you. When you walk through the fire you will not be burned, neither shall the flame kindle upon you.

May that promise be something in which you can lie down in peace, as you rest in the One who died and rose again to make it possible in your own heart and experience.

6

Isaiah 44:1-5

The Way of Revival

For I will pour water upon him that is thirsty, and floods upon the dry ground: I will pour my spirit upon thy seed, and my blessing upon thine offspring. (Isaiah 44:3)

One of the greatest perils of this hour, I believe, is that we Christians see our greatest problem as the titanic struggle between communism and the Western World, and that communism is regarded as our most dangerous enemy. We are inclined to equate Christianity and the Western World with everything that is good, and to equate evil with the Eastern World and everything that is communistic and bad. So somewhat piously we are inclined to assume that God is on our side, and that He is the avowed enemy of these so-called pagan and atheistic nations.

This is far from the truth, and it is also far from the real issue. There is something that is much deeper and more personal to us than that. In a word, it concerns the holiness of God and the sinfulness of the human heart. It is not a matter of nationalism, in which God is on our side and the devil on the other: it is rather a matter of personal repentance, of deep humiliation of heart before God. Our great enemy is not atheistic communism, but I would suggest to you that it is the lack of New Testament life and character that is being produced in the Christian church. It is not outward material enemies but inward spiritual breakdown. I believe with deep conviction that this is the issue

73

which confronts every one of us, and which is our primary concern in this tremendous hour of history.

"Surely God must see the righteousness of our cause," some people say.

But that which makes a righteous cause is a righteous people, and immediately, in saying that, the peril of our attitude is exposed. In the thinking of some people, it would be absolutely inconceivable to imagine that God would allow such a corrupt nation as Russia to humiliate so-called Western culture and Christianized civilization as it is found in Britain and the United States of America. But I would remind you that God has done that kind of thing before.

Allow me to recall a scriptural illustration before I come to grips with our text. The problem that confronted the prophet Habakkuk as he spoke to God was concerning the violence and corruption that were all around him, the lack of judgment and justice that were revealed in the world: therefore he asked the Lord for an explanation. The message he received only confounded him the more, for God said to him that He would raise up the evil, sinful power of the Chaldean Empire and use it to bring chastisement upon His people. Habakkuk's reply was, "But Lord, how can You do this? You are of purer eyes than to look upon sin. How can You possibly ally Yourself with a sinful people in order to bring judgment to bear?" He went up into his watchtower and waited for God's answer, and then it came: "If the vision tarry, wait for it. He whose soul is lifted up is not upright before me; but the just shall live by faith." In other words, right at the very heart of this people—God's people— were spiritual pride and self-righteousness. They were not, in fact, upright in character; and God went on to expose one judgment after another that He was going to bring to bear by using evil powers to do it, in order that He might humiliate His own people and bring them back in repentance to Himself.

The prayer of Habakkuk was, "O Lord, revive thy work in the midst of the years—[go on doing this, but] in wrath remember mercy" (Habakkuk 3:2). And when he saw what God was doing, his response was not to flood his generation with anti-Chaldean propaganda, but to make a trenchant appeal in the power of the Spirit of God for repentance and conviction of sin among the people of God.

This is the vital issue which confronts us today, and God only knows how much longer we may have to face it. The great call of the day is not for anticommunist propaganda or anticommunist hatred; it is for antisin behavior. The great call of the hour to our nations is a call to humiliation, to repentance before God, and to the forsaking of sin, which could yet turn the tide should God grant us His mercy.

It is just no answer for Christian people to sit back and say that the Lord is coming soon, all will be well! Remember that the New Testament, which bids us look eagerly for that day, to lift up our hearts for our redemption draws nigh, and speaks to us of the comfort and encouragement of the fact that the Lord Jesus Christ will come again, also tells such people to be prepared for battle and suffering, to humble themselves before God, to watch and to pray.

I would remind you of the trenchant words of the Apostle Peter: "Knowing this first, that there shall come in the last days scoffers, walking after their own lusts, And saying, Where is the promise of his coming? . . . But the day of the Lord will come as a thief in the night; in the which the heavens shall pass away with a great noise, and the elements shall melt with fervent heat. . . . Seeing then that all these things shall be dissolved [strange language, unthinkable fifty years ago, but not so now in the light of scientific discovery], what manner of persons ought ye to be in all holy conversation and godliness, Looking for and hasting unto the coming of the day of God, wherein the heavens being on fire shall be dissolved . . ." (2 Peter 3:3, 4, 10–12)?

Again, listen to Paul: "This know also, that in the last days perilous times shall come. For men shall be lovers of their own selves, covetous, boasters, proud, blasphemers, disobedient to parents, unthankful, unholy. . . . But evil men and seducers shall wax worse and worse. . . . But continue thou in the things which thou hast learned . . ." (2 Timothy 3:1, 2, 13, 14).

I repeat, it is just not good enough to sit under our heavenly bombproof shelter and say, "Jesus is coming back! There's a great day coming!" Rather it is to declare war against sin in the church—and out of it—that yet, before it is too late, God may have mercy upon us. It is so perilously easy for each of us to join the anticommunist army and to fail to face the appalling need and the desperate sin which are allowed to exist in our own lives, and to fail to appreciate the real, vital issue for every one of us in our relationship to the Lord Jesus.

Let me underline that it is only Holy Spirit power and fullness liberated through a repentant and humble church that can yet reverse the tide of history. The awful peril that surrounds us today is not that we should be swamped by communism, but that our self-righteous complacency should cut us off from the power of Almighty God, and we shall be left utterly bankrupt.

Now this principle is clearly revealed in the portion of Scripture which we are considering. See in the first place *the promise of revival.* "I will pour water upon him that is thirsty, and floods upon the dry gound: I will pour my spirit upon thy seed, and my blessing upon thine offspring" (Isaiah 44:3).

Here is the great covenant blessing of the church. Here is the gift of the Holy Spirit, the refreshing, life-giving water of which our Saviour spoke. The first promise of this text—"I will pour water upon him that is thirsty, and floods upon the dry ground" —is explained by the second—"I will pour my spirit upon thy seed, and my blessing upon thine offspring."

We must realize today that both the promise and the blessing have been fulfilled. The Holy Spirit came at Pentecost, and He has never been withdrawn. The greatest thing about a worship service is that He is in the midst of His people, and yet we have to acknowledge with shame that we are lamentably lacking in any evidence of His power.

If I understand my Bible right, and in a limited measure my own experience and certainly that of church history, when God works He works with the majesty of omnipotence. There is no mistaking the working of God. It cannot be explained; it can be imitated, but never reproduced. There is always a pathetic difference between the human efforts to engineer revival, and the God-sent showers from heaven that melt the heart. Without this and without Him we are like a ship without a breeze, like a battery without any spark to it, like a sacrificial offering in Old Testament days without the flame.

I cannot conceal this from my own heart, for I am often made to feel the humbling of my own spirit before God on this matter. You who serve the Lord in Sunday school, who go out witnessing to Him in prisons and hospitals and in the open air, who give out literature, you who in one way and another in different areas of your life seek to witness to Christ, don't you feel sometimes your impotence and powerlessness? Yet here is the promise of God that He will pour out water upon him that is thirsty. He will pour floods upon the dry ground. Oh, that He would open the windows of heaven now and pour us out a deluge of His grace! For our abounding sin and our satisfaction with ourselves need His abounding life and grace, His power and mercy.

Could we not, as we listen to God's Word, take His promise personally to our own hearts, plead it before the throne and say, "Lord, I present myself to Thee today. Here is Thy word; here is Thy promise. Here is the dry ground of my heart; I acknowledge it is desperately dry: do something in my life for Thy glory. Pour floods upon the dry ground!"

We can hear the truth constantly, and have the principle pointed out to us, but unless there is a moment when personally, alone with God, I go to Him and present to Him the emptiness of my heart and beseech Him to pour out of His fullness, nothing ever happens.

Here is God's promise of revival, but notice further *the product of revival*. There is a marvellous stamp of authentic permanence about the working of God: "And they shall spring up as among the grass, as willows by the water courses. One shall say, I am the Lord's; and another shall call himself by the name of Jacob; and another shall subscribe with his hand unto the Lord, and surname himself by the name of Israel" (v. 4, 5).

Wherever the Spirit of God comes, there will be life in the church and in the ministry. There will be life in prayer, in service, in holiness, and in testimony. There will be life in our love one toward another. Wherever the Holy Spirit is free and is given room, there is life, there is fullness, there is overflow.

All this has its outcome (as this text tells us) in the conversion of lives who are clear in their testimony and complete in their dedication: "One . . . shall call himself by the name of Jacob; and another shall subscribe with his hand unto the Lord, and sur-name himself by the name of Israel."

I tell you, I would give my life if only we might see that today! Oh, to hear not a few but hundreds say, "I am the Lord's!" and subscribe their hand to the Lord. That phrase is a reference to the custom of ancient times of a servant extending his hand that it might be branded with the name of his master. Oh, for the outpouring of the Holy Spirit which would bring that kind of thing about, and that in these present days we might see the tide turn!

In China there is "The Little Flock"; in Central Africa there is a group revitalized by the revival which began in Rwanda; in Assam in Northern India there is a little group living today in revival, and eighty percent of the whole area has been com-pletely turned to the Lord in the last few years. There are wonderful signs of blessing in many lands. In one area and another we can see the church of Jesus Christ put under pres-sure, under persecution and suffering, and I tell you, no matter what atheistic powers may seek to do to them, they are abso-lutely indestructible.

Then I think of the great nations of the West. With all our culture, with all our civilization, with all the saturation of the land with radio and television and the ministry of the Word of God, I look in vain to find any area where there is a significant moving of the Holy Spirit that one can call a real heaven-sent revival. Certainly there is the cloud the size of a man's hand seen in most unusual locations, but oh, for the floodtide, if it could please God, before the pressure is put on us in chastise-ment!

The promise of revival and the product of it: something per-manent, something unmistakably real, something dynamic, something lasting, something that cannot be shattered and cannot be scattered, and something that is absolutely indestructible. That is what we need today.

Look again at our text, and *the pathway of revival*. You don't have to wait for a great emotional experience. You don't have to wait for the gathering of a convention or a crowd. No, you just have to give twenty-four hours rugged, one hundred percent obedience to God's path of blessing, and you will live in revival even though everything around you is absolutely barren. Conventions may come and go, truths may be proclaimed, but if you fail to act upon that truth which is revealed to your heart until it ceases to be a truth that grips you, and you cease to be interested in it, one day you will stand before the Judgment Seat of Christ to be judged for it.

I notice in these verses that the promise of revival was against a background which was absolutely desperate in the story of the people of God. Because of disobedience and rebellion, because of their indifference and idolatry, He says, "Therefore I have profaned the princes of the sanctuary, and have given Jacob to the curse, and Israel to reproaches" (Isaiah 43:28).

Yet in such a day when God's people had rebelled and turned against Him, in such a day when judgment had been poured out upon them, there was still a pathway along which God was going to fulfill His promises.

I wonder if you have noticed that this is the only place in the whole of the Bible where the three names that God gave to His people Israel are put together: "Yet now hear, O *Jacob* my servant; and *Israel*, whom I have chosen . . . and thou, *Jesurun*, whom I have chosen" (v. 1, 2).

In this moment, when things had gone so completely wrong, when the people of God had sinned and were under His judgment because of it, He spoke to them and told them not to fear, and He brought together the three names that marked the distinctiveness of their lives and character.

Jacob, the name indicated the early days of the nation's life. Jacob was crafty and treacherous, cool and calculating and subtle, with a keen eye to his own interests. Selfish, shifty, unscrupulous Jacob! But in the midday of life there came an hour of deep dejection, an hour when he was driven out of dependence upon himself, when he felt around like a drowning man to clutch at any straw that would save him. Then there came an all-night conflict with God when, with weeping and supplication, he prevailed and received a new name, Israel, prince with God.

Jesurun, My righteous one, My upright one, the man whom I the Lord have taken from Jacob to be Jesurun, was a name that Jacob never bore in his own life. It pictured God's ideal for all His people at all times.

All of God's mercy and forgiveness in Jesus Christ is given to us in order that through our union with Him we may become like Him. And the road that takes a man from being Jacob and produces in him Jesurun is the road which takes him down through Peniel where, in brokenness of heart, in supplication and tears, God gives to him a new name and transforms his life. For the road from sin to purity, from selfishness to selflessness, from impunity to holiness, that road always leads down by the brook Jabbok, down to a midnight encounter when a man with a broken heart prevailed with God.

Have you ever been literally beaten out of all your confidence, and brought to a place of self-disgust and self-abandonment? Have you ever felt in your life that there is not one thing good in you, that you could rely on nothing, and there was nobody upon whom you could cling? Have you seen, at that moment through the dark when you were broken and desperate, the face of Jesus? Without that, the judgment of God applies to His church today as it did in the time of Habakkuk, when He said, "The soul of him that is lifted up within him is not upright within."

Here then is the promise of revival. Here is satisfaction for a thirsty soul, "I will pour . . . floods upon dry ground" (v. 3). Here is the one great need of this land today, and here is the path along which each Christian must tread: "I will not let Thee go, [Lord,] except Thou bless me" (Genesis 32:26). I verily believe that the course of history could be changed if the Christian church in our lands would repent of its self-sufficient program, would repent of making communism its target of attack, while it avoids the priority need of facing the deep sinfulness of the individual heart. Dare we do this? Oh that God would take you —if necessary alone, regardless of other people—from Jacob via Peniel to Jesurun today! He has to begin with somebody, or else it will be too late.

Would you pray this, "Lord, cure me of my intermittent piety, and make me consistent"? So John Wesley prayed. "Lord," he cried in his heart in the hour of great need, "make my religion to be my regular diet, and not medicine which I take as may be necessary!" He climaxed it alone with God one day on his face before an open Bible when he said, "Lord, don't let me go on another moment in any sin of which I have not thoroughly repented."

Would you dare to do that today? Do you know what would happen immediately in your situation? Some tongues of Christian people would undergo such a thorough, out-and-out revolutionary experience that others would scarcely recognize them as the same voices! The unkind, scathing, critical comment that is spoken behind the backs of fellow believers, in order to condemn them in the sight of others, would end. I believe that is one of the greatest hindrances to revival today, that somehow the fountain of our lips, which has brought out both blessing and cursing, would henceforth send out nothing that was bitter but everything that is sweet. That mind, which has been so ready to come to false judgment and to make false accusations, and to believe only the worst about a fellow Christian, would stop thinking that way, and would begin to love with the gentleness of Jesus Christ.

Dare you go up to someone in your church with whom you are not on speaking terms, and whose presence in the building makes you almost angry—dare you go up and say to him (or to her), "I'm sorry"?

I believe if God the Holy Ghost broke through into the church He would break through all our programs, our time-keeping and our schedules, and there would be hundreds of

Christians literally on their knees weeping and crying before God for revival. Some people through prejudice would be too proud to do it, but would *you* be ready to do that? Are you ready to meet God on that level today, to say you are sorry to one whom you have wronged, perhaps by a letter you wrote or things unkindly spoken? The pathway from Jacob to Jesurun takes you down by a broken heart to Peniel.

If you are saying you have no need of this message because you are not thirsty, I would say that such an attitude is one of the biggest hindrances to revival. I would go further, and say that God has nothing for you or for any self-sufficient person who says, "I don't need this."

Yes, *you* can have revival now; you can be the means in God's hand to spread the flame.

> I take salvation full and free,
> Through Him Who gave His life for me,
> He undertakes my all to be,
> "I take"—"He undertakes."
>
> I take the promised Holy Ghost,
> I take the power of Pentecost,
> To fill me to the uttermost
> "I take"—"He undertakes."
>
> I simply take Him at His word,
> I praise Him that my prayer is heard,
> I claim my answer from the Lord,
> "I take"—"He undertakes."
>
> A. B. SIMPSON

I quote from D. L. Moody: "One day in New York, oh, what a day! I cannot describe it, I seldom refer to it, it is almost too sacred an experience to name. I can only say that that day God revealed Himself to me. I had such an experience of His love that I had to ask Him to stay His hand. I went to preaching again. The sermons were no different. I didn't present any new truths but hundreds were converted, and I would not be placed back where I was before that blessed experience if you could give me all Glasgow."

I hope that some of you know that experience too. My heart bleeds for that increasingly in my own life. Listen to David Brainerd who, in the shade and a cool wind, wet with sweat as he prayed, was drawn out much from the world, grasping hold of God for multitudes of souls, and so preaching that scores of hardhearted, stoic Indian people were bowed down like grass before a scythe.

These men are giants, you say. Yes, but their God is *our God*, and they are only giants because they obeyed Him, and He made them strong out of weakness. God grant to this church, before it is too late, Holy Ghost revival, satisfaction for the thirsty heart, and that He will take you today to Peniel.

7

The Peril of Spiritual Idolatry

He feedeth on ashes: a deceived heart hath turned him aside, that he cannot deliver his soul, nor say, Is there not a lie in my right hand? (Isaiah 44:20).

The seventy years of captivity in Babylon, an entire span of human life, were designed in the hand of God to teach His people two outstanding lessons, which He could do no other way. The first, the all-sufficiency of Jehovah for every situation of life (v. 6–8); the second, the folly and sin of idolatry (v. 9–20).

As we consider the second lesson, the folly of idolatry, we are introduced in these verses to an idol factory of Isaiah's time with (if I may be so bold to add) a divine sarcasm which is withering in the extreme, and with a scorn of which only a holy God would be capable. From His viewpoint, we see the stupidity and futility of idol worship.

Watch the smith who is making an image out of molten metal (v. 12), but as he does so, he gets tired and thirsty. Quite clearly, therefore, he cannot possibly hope to produce something which could help other people in need. The effect is never any greater than the cause, and an idol cannot give strength to others when the one who makes it becomes exhausted in its manufacture!

Here, in verse 13, a carpenter is seen chiseling out a bit of wood into the figure of a man. This wood, you notice, has been taken from a tree which he or someone before him planted. He has taken part of the wood, stacked it, and made a fire to keep

85

him warm. The rest of it he fashions into an idol, before which he prostrates himself in worship. You can almost hear the chuckle of delight in the latter part of verse 16, when he warms himself by the fire. The next moment you see the same man before the same piece of wood in prayer, pleading with the remainder of the log, which he has not put into the fire, but which is made in the image of a man, to deliver him, as now it is his god!

Now, of course, our immediate reaction to that is to regard it as part of an outmoded civilization. You may see relics of it, perhaps, in the jungles of Africa or South America or other parts of the world, and insofar as the details of it are concerned, you would be right in taking that attitude and in coming to that conclusion. But insofar as the principles are concerned, if we take that attitude we are wrong; not merely are we wrong, but dangerously wrong.

We wonder how any man could be so inconceivably stupid. We would admit, of course, that a very large percentage of our population use images of stone or wood, or even plastic, as charms in their cars which help, so they claim, to fix their thought in prayer. I do not think the prophet would have anything to do with that theory. He would affirm that for the mass of people it is absolute fiction, and that worship stops at what a man sees or what he touches. Oh, yes, there is a lot of visible equivalent to idol worship which is not too remote, and that is what is described for us in Isaiah 44.

There is, however, an even more serious peril which—and I say it with a sense of awe and deep conviction—unless we repent, is going to involve multitudes of this generation facing the challenge of martyrdom under world communism.

I quote from an article: "The hour is late. There are few signs of repentance in America [this could apply equally well to the whole Western World]. With the enemy at our gates, this Christian country still insists on yet a little sleep, a little slumber, a little folding of the hands. As a nation we have succumbed to the opiates of sensual pleasure and entertainment, injected into our bloodstream by the 'reds' of Hollywood. We are absorbed in wealth, comfort, ease, luxury, and a high standard of living. Theaters, television, sport, and sex have us so enchanted that we are walking right into the jaws of our charmer from Moscow. Even the people of God, in many instances, are so enamoured with money and material things—with new cars and new furniture, with the latest modern gadgets, with television—that they have become practically stupified and almost completely ineffective in the spiritual life."

That is a very serious indictment, but we cannot escape the truth of it. "Judgment must begin at the house of God" (1 Peter 4:17), says Peter, and therefore repentance must begin among God's people if there is to be a spiritual awakening, a quickening of spiritual life which alone can reverse the disastrous trend of history.

It took seventy years of captivity in Babylon to teach Israel the folly of idolatry. Do you and I ever stop to ask ourselves, I wonder what it is going to take to teach us? Oh, that we may see for ouselves this principle individually, and its implications personally, while there is time!

I remind you that it is not what a man *makes* that becomes his idol, but what he *worships.* If the worship of a human heart is given to anything less than the revelation of God in the person of Jesus Christ, immediately you set up in that life the principle of idol worship. As Paul says in Romans 1:25, we begin to serve the creature more than the Creator. This is the essence of idolatry, and it is enforced by the words of the apostle in Colossians 3:5 where he says, "[Beware of] covetousness, which is idolatry."

Very well then, here is the equivalent in modern form of what is pictured for us in Isaiah 44. Of course, it takes a different form and has a greater measure of refinement, but it is no less deadly in its effect, and no less sure of the judgment of the living God. To be made aware of it is one thing, but to deal with it as it may exist personally in my life in the presence of God is another, and it is this, in the name of the Lord, I would seek to call us to do now.

To help us to do this, look attentively at the whole sweep of this principle of spiritual idolatry as we see it described for us here.

"He feedeth on ashes: a deceived heart hath turned him aside, that he cannot deliver his soul, nor say, Is there not a lie in my right hand?" (v. 20).

This is the description of a man who comes under the indictment of a holy God in terms of the quality of life he is living. A deceived heart has turned him aside so that he cannot deliver his soul.

As we consider these fundamental principles, please be honest and open with yourself before the Lord, as you in quietness study this passage of Scripture.

Quite clearly here is the practice of idolatry: "He feedeth on ashes." Food is essential, because hunger and appetite are universal. As a man's body needs food, so his mind demands truth and his soul needs God. That is why a man is different from any other creature on the earth. It is true of all men everywhere. This material world cannot possibly satisfy a creature who is made specifically for the enjoyment of fellowship with God. When, as in the case of Solomon as an example, life is filled with everything wealth and power can give, when a man who has all that turns from it, as a vain, empty thing, a mere mirage—surely that proves that the human race belongs to something more than merely material things of time. The body needs food for strength and sustenance; it needs food to keep us warm; it needs food in order that we might grow. Similarly, the soul within the body needs God for spiritual life and energy and strength. It needs God for warmth of fellowship and love, the only love that can really satisfy. The human soul needs God that he might grow in the likeness of Jesus Christ and be fashioned into that likeness.

Yes, both body and soul need food, and the moment a man begins to feed on God he begins to feed on the One, the Lord Jesus, who said, "I am the living bread which came down from heaven: if any man eat of this bread, he shall live for ever: and the bread that I will give is my flesh, which I will give for the life of the world" (John 6:51).

Again He said, ". . . I am the bread of life: he that cometh to me shall never hunger; and he that believeth on me shall never thirst" (John 6:35).

It is Christ, and He alone, who satisfies the human heart. The appetite, the God-given appetite of every life, is satisfied completely, perfectly, and solely in the Lord Jesus. Yet there are millions of people with such needs who have been converted and are feeding, as Isaiah says, on ashes, spending money for that which is not bread and labor for that which does not satisfy.

Let me press this point. The man who is sensual tries to satisfy the hunger for love with the ashes of physical satisfaction, and he finds himself utterly deluded. He has an overstimulated appetite, and he uses the God-given appetite of the body in a perverted way as he feeds on ashes, and makes sex his god. The man of the world who worships money and position will sacrifice anything in order to achieve what is called a "status symbol." That is why he must have his new car, the latest stereophonic hi-fi. That is why he must have his beautiful home and expensive clothes. All to satisfy the inward desire to establish a status in the eyes of people, because they worship the god of this world.

There is the student who at the university begins to doubt and question the very existence of God, and he feeds upon the ashes of human learning and human opinion. His appetite was intended to be nourished by the truth of God.

So we could go on, but enough has been said to show that, in one form or another these substitutes for God, with which men seek to satisfy themselves everywhere, are as incapable of satisfying the heart as ashes would meet the hunger of the body.

Here is the modern practice of idolatry, and it is not far removed from us. It is neither remote nor historic, but is something that is going on now all around us; and maybe you have found yourself somewhere in that picture.

Reading the text again we see not only the practice of idolatry but the tremendous power of it. The veil is lifted and we are shown beneath the surface as we read, "A deceived heart hath turned him aside, that he cannot deliver his soul" (Isaiah 44:20).

Here is the source of the problem. The Scripture tells us that the devil is the great deceiver of man, and the Lord Jesus told us in Matthew 24:24, "if it were possible, [he] shall deceive the very elect." Satan always puts a gloss on things and represents as utterly desirable that which the Bible states is totally sinful. He gives it a wonderful attraction and carefully hides from us what happens when we grasp that which he offers. He is the great deceiver of men. How clever he is in assuring that there is no painful consequence that can ever happen to us as long as we follow his suggestion.

"It's natural! It's God-given!" he whispers in our ears, and he refuses to admit the possibility that the God-given appetite could be exercised in a wrong way.

So a deceived heart turns aside the whole man; it blinds his understanding, it biases his will, and persuades him of the attractiveness of the road that Satan opens up. That is exactly what verses 18 and 19 of Isaiah 44 are saying:

"They have not known nor understood: for he hath shut their eyes, that they cannot see; and their hearts, that they cannot understand. And none considereth in his heart, neither is there knowledge nor understanding to say, I have burned part of it in the fire; yea, also I have baked bread upon the coals thereof; I have roasted flesh, and eaten it: and shall I make the residue thereof an abomination? shall I fall down to the stock of a tree?"

The heart of man, says Jeremiah, is deceitful above all things and desperately wicked. I am sure that each of us, at one time or another, has been drawn away from the dictate of a better judgment to obey the persistence of an evil desire. You remember the language of James 1:14, 15, "But every man is tempted, when he is drawn away of his own lust, and enticed. Then when lust hath conceived, it bringeth forth sin: and sin, when it is finished, bringeth forth death."

Now this is true of every form of idolatry, of everything which removes God from the place of worship in the human heart. It is equally true of the self-indulgent kind of life about which I have been speaking, and it is true of the man who perverts his physical appetite. Every form of idolatry operates in the human heart with devastating power and with tremendous control.

Look further in the text at the penetration of idolatry in life: "he cannot deliver his soul, nor say, Is there not a lie in my right hand?" (Isaiah 44:20).

At some time or another, in the life of a man who has pursued this path, there have been moments when he has longed with all his heart to flee from the bondage of it, when he has awakened after having practiced it to see the disaster facing him. Suddenly he sees the course along which he is being taken, and realizes in a flash the emptiness of it. With purposeful heart he decides to turn back to God, but now he finds that the deeply rooted habits are too strong for him. Jeremiah's words have been proved true: "Can the Ethiopian change his skin, or the leopard his spots? then may ye also do good, that are accustomed to do evil" (Jeremiah 13:23).

In your life, was it a time of sickness when you seriously made an attempt to break with idolatry? Or was it a time of bereavement, when you stood and wept at the grave of one who was dear to you, and vowed in the presence of God that your life would be different? I wonder. But in the case of sickness or bereavement, your heart was melted before God, and you wept; now restored strength and the passage of time have hardened you again.

I have seen many a man broken and in tears in time of physical or emotional weakness, then when he is back on his feet again and one hundred percent fit, he is as tough as nails. How easily changing circumstances can alter our attitude to life and eternity!

The Lord Jesus told a remarkable parable in Luke 11:21, 22, in which He likens Satan to a strong man armed, keeping his palace and his goods in safety, and his servants did not realize the extent of their bondage. They are lulled into a false sense of security and peace until, as Paul says in 1 Thessalonians chapter 5, sudden destruction comes upon them. Is it not amazing that rational human beings should be so insensible, in the midst of such danger, and against all the dictates of better judgment? For sin is irrational, idolatry is folly, so much so indeed that those caught in the web are unable to recognize there is a lie in their right hand.

I want to ask you a very simple question, and only God can help you to answer it. The right hand in Scripture and in many other areas of life is always the symbol of power and authority and service. What do you hold in your right hand today? That before which you worship, the throne before which you bend, is it a lie? Many a professing Christian has lost all sensitiveness to God, all desire to pray, all appetite for His Word, all concern for the winning of others, because he holds a lie in his right hand. Oh, the penetration of idolatry!

The glory of this message, however, is found in what I would call the protection from idolatry, for if you cast your eye down Isaiah 44:22 there is a wonderful silver lining to be found, where God says, "I have blotted out, as a thick cloud, thy transgressions, and, as a cloud, thy sins: return unto me; for I have redeemed thee."

Bless the Lord! There is a strong man armed who has enslaved us, but Scripture tells us that there is a Stronger than he, who has overcome and taken from him all his armor in which he trusted, and divided his spoil.

Do you remember the very first sermon the Lord Jesus preached? He spoke of proclaiming liberty to the captive and the opening of the prison to them that are bound. If you are one today who has been feeding on ashes in one area or another in your life, you need do so no longer. A deceived heart need turn you aside no more. Though past idolatry has involved you in guilt, let me say to you that the sufficiency of the blood of Jesus Christ will cleanse you from all sin. If that penetration seems so deep that there is no relief, the grace of God is always sufficient.

"For the flesh lusteth against the Spirit, and the Spirit against the flesh" (Galatians 5:17), and that will always be true. Satan will always have power to tempt, and the carnal heart will always be prone to lapse back again into carnality. Yet the Word of God tells you that when you come to Jesus there is One greater in you than he that is in the world. It is through the death on the cross that our Lord has become food for our lives: "Jesus said unto them, Verily, verily, I say unto you, Except ye eat the flesh of the Son of man, and drink his blood, ye have no life in you. Whoso eateth my flesh, and drinketh my blood, hath eternal life; and I will raise him up at the last day. For my flesh is meat indeed, and my blood is drink indeed. He that eateth my flesh, and drinketh my blood, dwelleth in me, and I in him" (John 6:53–56).

It is a tremendous thing to know that someone who has been feeding on ashes, and in whose life there has come one form of idolatry after another, may begin to feed on Jesus Christ by faith in the heart. You can begin to think about Him and all He has done for you. You may receive Him into your heart and make Him real in your life by personal appropriation. You may believe that you have received Him, and go on to possess Him, and so feed on and live by the resurrection life of the living Lord Jesus.

If this would be the purpose of your heart, which means essentially the dropping of the idol from your right hand, then it must go immediately.

I am sure that this is the only effective counterattack that our free world can have against communism today. I do not make this the motive for turning to God, for receiving Christ and living for Him—God forbid! But I would say this, that while at present in world affairs we talk and protest and deplore, we go on retreating and suffering defeat, why should not a mighty spiritual surge of life in the Holy Spirit awaken the whole Christian church and every professing child of God in the free world? Why should it not drive back this evil monster that nothing else can? There is only one thing that stops such a movement of the Spirit: it is that which you hold in your right hand. Satan has so deluded you that you don't see that it is a lie, a false confidence, and a delusion, because it is something so attractive.

Am I not hitting the nail on the head in saying that the lie in your right hand has led to prayerlessness and ineffectiveness, to a deadly formal religious experience? You have lost through it all spiritual sensitivity, and so prayer meetings languish, and concern for men and women without God is practically nonexistent. All the things that God intends for His people lie today, in so many hearts, buried under the ashes of a deeper devotion to the home, television, stereo, the car, the maintaining of status, and so on. All that which God intends to be our portion —God-given appetites satisfied with a God-given response to His will in prayer, in devotion, and in testimony—are buried under a heap of ashes.

One day God averted the judgment of Nineveh because the people, from the king down, turned to Him in fasting, prayer, and repentance. God is just the same today, and He can still bring the counsels of the heathen to naught. He still says, "If my people, which are called by my name, shall humble themselves, and pray, and seek my face, and turn from their wicked ways; then will I hear from heaven, and will forgive their sin, and will heal their land" (2 Chronicles 7:14). He is still saying that to us: "*If* my people . . ."

What is in your right hand?

What do you think would happen if we held up to God our right hand with the idol which we have been worshiping, and told Him, "Lord Jesus, I trust You today to remove this, and I am willing that it might go"?

For one thing, prayer would take priority in your life. For another, money would be released for the Lord's work. Luxuries would not be desired—indeed some of them would be promptly sold, and the proceeds given to the spread of the gospel.

Witnessing to neighbors across the street would be a normal expression of the love of God shed abroad in the heart. It would mean less time chatting with friends and more time in the Word of God. It would mean less time socializing and more time evangelizing. It would mean that the whole church would come alive with spiritual power and liberty and vitality, and would be an effective instrument in the hand of God for revival.

"Lord, I come to You with empty hands and an empty heart. I yield myself to You completely, and with a deep desire that

I may be available to You for whatever You desire, or wherever You wish to send me. Lord, I have determined in my heart today to feed on the living Christ, and to trust the Holy Spirit for power to show heaven and earth and hell that I mean business in this. The prayer of my heart is, O send a great revival, Lord, and let it now begin in me!"

8

Isaiah 44:21–28

God Can Forgive Anything Except . . .

I have blotted out, as a thick cloud, thy transgressions, and, as a cloud, thy sins: return unto me; for I have redeemed thee. (Isaiah 44:22)

Isaiah is always known by every Bible student as the evangelical prophet. That is not only because of what he had to say about the coming of the Lord Jesus, but because running right through his prophecy there is the gospel of the grace of God which it is our delight to preach and to know. Over and over again it stands out so clearly, and perhaps nowhere more so than in the verse which is our text.

I do not know your circumstances, but some maybe are puzzled regarding the future and seek guidance. Others are facing tremendous problems and feeling desperately weak, and need strength. There are a multitude of pressures and needs, but let me say that the greatest need of everyone primarily is forgiveness, first that we might meet with God on the question of sin, and have His forgiving mercy in our hearts. It is out of this that there begins to flow all the other things of which we are so consciously in need.

Some would say that forgiveness is impossible because God's laws are unchangeable. Others would say that forgiveness is inevitable because God is a God of love. The Bible says that forgiveness is a miracle which only God Himself could accomplish, and I want to speak about the forgiving mercy of God in our lives. We will fasten upon this verse entirely, and I want to take from it some thoughts which I trust may help us as we seek to understand God's goodness and His forgiving grace.

First of all, we see that sin has some basic definite characteristics. There are two words used here which, if I understand the Bible meaning of them, I come to comprehend something of what sin really is.

Transgressions is the first word meaning rebellion, the rising up of my rebellious will not merely against the law, but against the God who gave the law.

When you think about it, it makes all the difference whether you consider sin from this angle solely on the surface—so that when you and I do something that is wrong we say, "Well, I know this is wrong," and leave it at that—or whether we get beneath the surface and go right down to the depths. There we recognize that the worst part of it all is that I—little, puny, insignificant being—am lifting up my pride, my will, against God who made me, and saying to Him, "Did I hear You say to me, Thou shalt not? Well, my answer to You is, I will. Or did I hear You say to me, Thou shalt? Then my answer is, I will not." This is transgression. Understanding it from that aspect it does not make much difference whether we call sin big or small; it eliminates that distinction altogether, for this verse tells me (and the whole Bible reveals the truth) that sin is bascially rebellion against an omnipotent and almighty God.

The second word is *sin,* and the meaning of the Hebrew used here is *missing the mark,* a failure to attain a purpose, like an arrow not being quite on target. The same idea is conveyed in Romans 3:22, 23: for there is no difference: "For all have sinned, and come short of the glory of God." Come short of what? The glory of God. And what is that?

The writer to the Hebrews says of our Lord that He is the express image of His person, the brightness of His glory, the outshining of the glory of God. Just as the light that comes down from the sun is the same nature as the sun itself, so the Lord Jesus is the outshining, the revealing of the glory of God.

If you are honest and brave enough to put your life alongside the life of the One who is the glory of God, Jesus Himself, you will never again argue with the fact of sin. You will acknowledge that you have come short of Him.

Here, then, sin has essential characteristics: this is how the Bible defines it. In the first place it is rebellion, and in the second place it is a missing of the mark. The one, of course, comes from the other. Rebellion is the root of it; and because I have rebelled against God then, as the outcome of it, my life misses the mark, it falls short of God's purpose.

Do you recognize these failures in your life, and are you willing to acknowledge them in the presence of God: that you have been rebellious, and that your life does indeed come short of the glory of God as seen in the Lord Jesus Christ?

Isaiah 44:22 implies further that sin leaves a permanent record: "I have blotted out. . . ."

That simple statement suggests a book, a record, if you like. It has been my habit for many years to keep a personal diary. Maybe you do the same. I have kept it now for some twenty-five years or more, and I can look back over those years and know exactly where I was and what I was doing on any particular day in any particular year. That may seem to you to be of little advantage, but it is interesting. When you get to a certain time of life you begin doing that kind of thing, I suppose—you look back. I am quite sure, however, that if your diary is anything like mine, you don't put some of the unpleasant things in it. You recall the matters you like to remember, those that were pleasant. Of course, there were some things that were very unpleasant, but you do not record them. There were also some things you said or did to others which were unkind or ungracious, where you sinned grievously, but these are never entered into a diary. No, it is, at best, only a fragmentary record.

"I have blotted out . . ." says the Lord. This suggests a record of a different kind, a writing that is totally unlike my fragmentary story of life, because the plain fact is (and the Bible teaches it) that each one of us is writing a daily biography. It is being written in invisible ink, but in indelible ink also. We read it now vaguely, indistinctly, and this diary which we are writing is being filed for future reference in heaven. It is our own hand that is writing it, and it is God's knowledge, understanding, and omniscience that is recording it. We write it day by day, moment by moment, indelibly, invisibly, by the life we live.

It is a very solemn thing, but nothing you or I do ever dies; it lives! Everything I do—every thought, every action—becomes part of me, and of my life. It doesn't die but lives on. Our lives bear the imprint; God writes it carefully down; and one day you and I will be complete in His presence. Do you say that is very fanciful?

I would remind you of Revelation 20:12, where a dramatic scene is brought before us. There John is given a vision into the future: "And I saw the dead, small and great, stand before God; and the books were opened. . . ."

"Stand before God"—what solemn words they are!

Now, today, you may stand physically and mentally, but spiritually you may, colloquially speaking, be flat on your back. But one day the dead shall stand, the body merely decayed into dust and ashes, but the spirit going right on until it is called into the immediate presence of God.

The books are opened, and the dead are judged out of the book according to their works. When a man faces that indictment, it will be impossible for him to disown his own handwriting. It will be the infallible, complete, absolute, final record in truth, without any possible miscarriage of justice, without any possible half-truth. It will reveal all the facts and the whole story.

Sin leaves a permanent record. We may try to hide it, escape from it, forget it, explain it, excuse it, run away from it, change our location, move to other circumstances—to another land or area or city—to try to start all over again: but sin is indelible. It may be written in invisible ink, but the record is there, kept for future reference. "I have blotted out. . . ."

The verse suggests also that sin has a darkening power: "I have blotted out, as a thick cloud . . ." and that reveals darkness between the soul and God.

I am sure you have been out many times on a lovely sunny

day in the country, and as you enjoyed the sunshine and warmth, suddenly before the day was over the clouds began to gather, and a dark cloud blotted out the sun. What happened? The birds stopped singing, the flowers began to close up, and there was a strange, eerie sort of silence as everything became dark.

Sin does that: it shuts out the glory. "But your iniquities have separated between you and your God, and your sins have hid his face from you . . ." (Isaiah 59:2).

It is just impossible for a man or a woman who is in rebellion against God ever to have fellowship with Him, or even to see His face while they maintain that attitude. Every evil, every sin blots out the face of God from our vision. Whether a man's sin be from the ugly swamp of impurity, or whether it be the more refined, but equally ugly, area of self-righteousness, all blots out the face of God. Sin has devastatingly darkening powers. Sin has a way of darkening the soul and separating it from the way of life. If that is true now, it is even more true in eternity. You remember the parable the Lord Jesus told as He spoke about our accountability to God. He dealt with one man who had buried his talent and whom He called an unprofitable servant, and said of him that he should be cast into outer darkness.

If you desire any further evidence of it, you have only to think with me of a place called Calvary where God in Christ reconciled the world to Himself. At the moment of His accomplishment, as the sin of the whole human race was imputed to Him, He cried, "My God, my God, why hast thou forsaken me?" (Matthew 27:46). He cried out of an impenetrable darkness, for through three hours of that noonday there was complete and utter blackness as the sun hid its face as He, the Saviour of the world, bore our sins.

Sin has a darkening effect. I believe many of you know about that. Perhaps some of you are not Christians, and God is unreal to you as you never get through to Him. Of course not! You may be a Christian, and you do know the Lord, but somehow things have got between you and Jesus, and there is a dark cloud between. That can happen at any time to all of us. There is nothing more certain to hide the face of God than the fact of sin from which we refuse to break.

Sin leaves a permanent record, it has a devastating and darkening power, but this verse also suggests it can be removed: "I have blotted out" suggests the erasing of the record altogether. "I have blotted out, as a thick cloud" suggests the removal of the darkness.

The two things that sin does are dealt with: the record is erased, and the cloud which hides God from us has been swept away.

Yes, here is the promise of a tremendous possibility. That blurred and stained page of life can be canceled. The New Testament tells us that the blood of Jesus Christ, God's Son, cleanses us from all sin. We may spend our years as a tale that is told, and what is written is written. The record can be removed as if it had never happened. All of it may be blotted out.

Furthermore, the cloud can be swept away, for the sun which shines above it can shine with such force, and the love of God can be so powerful, that it penetrates right through to the depths. The clouds can be swept away by the matchless love of God in Jesus Christ our Lord. There is a tremendous thought that the Ethiopian cannot change his skin, nor the leopard his spots. How impossible it is for that to happen; but the blood of Jesus does not only cleanse the skin, but it changes the heart, and goes down to the very depths of our need.

That is the gospel truth. This is the truth of forgiveness, and unless we know it, we may well be amazed at the absolute wonder that God could ever pardon the sin of a human heart. But He can, and He has.

The Bible takes hold of all kinds of human character and failure, and places them into one single condition of guilt, need, helplessness. It recognizes only two kinds of people in all the universe: those who have had their sins forgiven, and those who have not. There are people who are saved, and those who are lost. In this area there is no neutral ground; and similarly the

Bible recognizes only two conditions beyond this life, heaven and hell. There is no neutral ground. The Word of God brings the whole of existence into one simple, straightforward situation in which all have sinned, and therefore all are guilty. But there is a way of life and salvation by which all may be saved. The matchless grace of God begins right down at the very depths of our need as He says, ". . . return unto me; for I have redeemed thee" (Isaiah 44:22). Sin can be removed.

There is one other thing, and perhaps it is the most important of all here. Sin is removed by a miracle.

Now our text has revealed to us some of the characteristics of sin, that it is rebellion, a falling short of God's purpose and plan. It leaves a record which is one day going to be set before the throne of God unless it is dealt with in life right now. That which we have forgotten God will speak to us about on that day before His throne. Sin leaves a mark, it darkens the view of God, and makes fellowship and communion with Him impossible. It kills our prayer and Bible reading, making these things meaningless. It does all this, but it can be removed. The question is, how? My answer is that sin is removed by a miracle of forgiveness.

What a difference it makes to be forgiven! You see, a forgiven man is one who has had his relationship with God altered. No longer does he hide from Him, but he is welcomed in His presence as His child. He has been forgiven, and this transforms everything. The forgiven man is introduced into a relationship with God which makes all the difference, not only to that relationship, but to every other relationship in life.

I wonder if you have stopped to realize that, if you are wrong with God, you are wrong everywhere else. If you are out of touch with Him, then you are out of touch with others, and nothing goes right. If you do not have Him, you do not have anything. There is no meaning in anything for you.

The stupendous miracle of forgiveness is expressed best in the words of the Reverend Wade Robinson.

Heaven above is softer blue,
Earth around is sweeter green!
Something lives in every hue
Christless eyes have never seen:
Birds with gladder songs o'er-flow,
Flowers with deeper beauties shine,
Since I know, as now I know,
I am His, and He is mine.

What a difference this miracle makes! It changes our relationship with God; it changes our relationship with everyone else.

What obstacles forgiveness overcomes! You see, to forgive a man, and yet to uphold the moral law of the universe, is a miracle which only God can do. That is something you can neither do nor understand except when you see it at Calvary. As you examine the sacrifices mentioned in the Bible you find that, apart from the fact that they were animal sacrifices, that life offered on the cross was a man, a God-man. There is this one great difference: all previous sacrifices were those of a guilty conscience; the sacrifice of Jesus on the cross was the redemption of the love of God. This was something so entirely different.

The cross tells me what God thinks of sin. He condemns it altogether, yet He proclaims free and absolute pardon for every one of us. Forgiven by a miracle, and yet the moral law of God is upheld. Forgiven at infinite cost, and forgiven so freely.

If I want to know what it cost God to forgive my sin I must look at the cross, and as I measure the cost of forgiveness then I marvel all the more what it has cost Him to set a sinner free.

Oh, what obstacles are overcome in the miracle of forgiveness! God has upheld His law, broken through and stooped down to the most sinful, degraded life, and lifted it up into His very presence. He does so, and yet retains His integrity. This is only possible because the sword of His justice is buried in the heart of His Son.

How full is our forgiveness! When God forgives, there are no half measures. When people forgive us, or when we forgive others, there are often reservations in mind. "I don't trust that

person any more!" we say to ourselves. You are not sure
whether you ought to do it, and so you delay. Perhaps there is
suspicion, and you will find yourself reminding the other person
of past failure. Our forgiveness can be so condescending; we
feel we are exercising real virtue.

The Apostle Peter felt this one time when he asked Jesus,
"Lord, how often shall I forgive my brother? Seven times?"
"No," replied the Lord, "four hundred and ninety times!" In
other words, stop measuring the limit of your forgiveness. You
are to forgive others in the same limitless measure that Christ
forgave you. When we forgive there are often mental reservations, and a failure to forget the past.

When God forgives He does not say, "Return to me, *and* I will
redeem you." He says, "Return to me, *for I have* redeemed
thee."

The very day I come He removes all the burden of past
failure, and immediately He lays upon me the burden of Christian responsibility. He takes away one burden and lays on another.

The old life with all its weaknesses and sins has suddenly died
off, although we are very conscious it is still there. It is amazing
that the very moment when I come to God in Jesus Christ—
though the previous day I may have denied and rejected Him,
proved untrue and unfaithful, and blasphemed Him—that very
moment of forgiveness is the moment when He offers me a task
that angels in heaven would delight to do. Oh, how full is the
forgiveness of God! His immediate forgiveness and mercy are
followed by the immediate commission to go into all the world
to preach the gospel to every creature, and all past sin and
failure is buried in the oblivion of God's forgetfulness.

Further, how free is God's forgiveness! All we have to do is
to take it with the outstretched hand of a receiving faith, and
not wait to be worthy. God takes all the risks in forgiving us in
a way that only His love can do. He invites us to take His free
forgiveness now. If I long for this with all my heart, that is a sure
sign to God that I am ashamed of the past. If I long for His
forgiveness and cleansing, that is an evidence to heaven that I

yearn to be free of all that has been part of me in the years that have gone, and at that moment He is at hand with His gift.

You can never deserve God, but you can accept Him. You can never merit His love and His life, but you can receive Him. This is the only way that men, whether they live on the Gold Coast or on Skid Row, can come together, for they meet the Lord on the same level in the same place, at the foot of the cross, equally guilty in the sight of heaven. There they will receive immediately the cleansing power of the blood of Christ, and are commissioned to serve the King of kings. That is God's way of forgiveness. It doesn't leave our pride a leg to stand on, and it brings us right down at the foot of Calvary. Oh, how free is God's forgiveness!

Finally, how inclusive is God's forgiveness! We read in Psalm 103:3 that He is the One "Who forgiveth all thine iniquities. . . ." I need to pause there because someone might be saying, "Yes, I go along with you, but I am sure He cannot forgive THAT"—and you know what THAT is: the thing you didn't put in your diary, of which as you go back over the years you are bitterly ashamed, and it has left its mark upon your life, and its stain upon your character.

"Do you mean to tell me that God can even get down so low as to forgive THAT?" Yes, I do, for He forgives *all* your iniquities.

Listen to the music of 1 John 1:7, "if we walk in the light, as he is in the light, we have fellowship one with another, and the blood of Jesus Christ his Son cleanseth us from all sin."

Then is there no exception to God's forgiveness? Yes, there is. Do you mean to tell me there is a question mark as to the limit of His forgiving mercy? Yes, just one.

It is not the character of my sin, nor the depth or length of it; it is not the tenacity of its hold upon me, nor the shame and degradation of it, because God is able to forgive all that. Then where is the exception?

"But if we walk in the light . . . If we confess our sins, he is faithful and just to forgive us our sins, and to cleanse us from all unrighteousness" (v. 7, 9). Let this burn its way into your heart today: sin to be forgiven must be forsaken.

It would have been easier to put that record down in the diary of your life if, at the time you wrote it, you knew it was being forsaken. Maybe you don't have to go back so many years to recall it because, though it is not written in the record book on earth it is written in heaven, and the trouble is it has never been basically forsaken. There is no forgiveness unless there is a forsaking of sin right now. I tell you, I would not dare enter the presence of God with an unconfessed sin upon my heart and conscience, loading and weighing me down as a guilty soul.

What I confess, He will forgive. What He forgives, He will cleanse. Then that vessel of a human heart that He cleanses He will fill with His Spirit, and what He fills, He will use.

9

Isaiah 45:1-4

Treasures of Darkness

And I will give thee the treasures of darkness, and hidden riches of secret places, that thou mayest know that I, the Lord, which call thee by thy name, am the God of Israel. (Isaiah 45:3)

In order that we might receive all that God has for us in this verse in its spiritual application to our own lives, let us consider first its literal meaning and its historical application.

These are words that were actually spoken by Jehovah the living God to a heathen king, Cyrus King of Persia. This is the only place in Scripture where a man who was an unbeliever is called the anointed of God (v. 1). He was given that title because, even though he did not realize it himself, he was to be God's chosen instrument through whom the people of Israel were to be delivered from captivity. Just as at one time the Lord used the mighty power of Chaldea to bring chastisement, judgment, and captivity upon His people, so He will use yet another heathen power as an instrument to set His people free. In all the dynamic rise and fall of kings, thrones, and empires, one after another, behind the outward events which any casual observer could see, there was the unseen hand of an Omnipotent God, directing all the affairs of men and nations for one supreme object, the deliverance of His people. "For Jacob my servant's sake, and Israel mine elect, I have even called thee by thy

name: I have surnamed thee, though thou hast not known me"
(v. 4).

This is not only a fact of history. It is the story of all history
which might well be called His story. It is the truth behind the
breathtaking events of the decade in which we now live. Cyrus
is preferred in order that Israel might be released. Cyrus shall
have a kingdom, but only in order that God's people may have
their liberty. The Lord raises up one, and He puts down another. Behind all the drama of human events today there is a
God who is planning for His church—through affliction and
persecution, chastening and tribulation—to be perfected and
prepared to inherit the Kingdom of God.

In the early days of the Christian church, when Paul and
Barnabas were conserving those who were converted to the
Christian faith as they went from place to place, confirming
them in their faith and exhorting them to remain steadfast, they
reminded them that it was through much tribulation they
would inherit the Kingdom of God. He, our Lord Jesus, who
sold all that He had to purchase a pearl of great price, His
church, is pressing that pearl through the fiery furnace of persecution so that one day, having been used to turn many to righteousness, as the Book of Daniel says, it may shine as the brightness of the firmament, and as the stars for ever and ever.

You will be kept sane only as you hold that truth deep down
in your heart and mind today. If you have that truth gripping
your soul, then in the midst of all tribulation you will have
peace.

To return to our text: at the time when it was spoken, Babylon
was immensely powerful. We are told that it was forty-five miles
in circumference, it had walls thirty-two feet thick, so wide that
six chariots could proceed side by side and drive abreast on
them. Those walls were one hundred cubits high, and within
that vast citadel, like an enormous concentration camp, the
Israelites were captive for seventy years. But God would deliver
them from that bondage. So these promises were given to the
one whom He had chosen to use as His instrument for their

salvation. The history of their subsequent deliverance is given in Daniel 5.

At the time Isaiah spoke to the people of Israel nothing would seem more improbable. There were, of course, evidences that the chastisement of God was of necessity leading His people into captivity, but in a mere two hundred years all that was said here was fulfilled and accomplished because God raised up a heathen power in order to do His will.

I have no doubt whatsoever, of course, that God could have done this through one of His own people, a Jew. He could have done it, for instance, through Zerrubabel, governor of Judah, who after the captivity laid the foundations of the new temple.

May I suggest to you that never in all history has God trusted His people with a vast amount of material resources and material power? God does not operate in that way. Very seldom has the Christian church been blessed with wealth, as the world counts wealth. God knows the snares and temptations that are attached to such, and so He has seldom seen fit to entrust His people with it. Rather He has made good use of it in the hands of other people for the good of His own, by making friends of the mammon of unrighteousness.

So for the sake of His people He will hold the right hand of Cyrus (Isaiah 45:1). He will subdue nations before him, and He will loose the loins of kings. That strange phrase means that He will terrify them! In Daniel 5, Belshazzar at the drunken feast saw writing on the wall, and we are told that his loins were loosed and his knees smote one against the other in terror!

Cities would surrender to Cyrus, gates would open before him, the long distance marches apparently would be made easy, as God made the crooked places straight in front of him. No opposition would be able to stand in his way, and even gates of brass with bars of iron (of which there were no less than one hundred in Babylon) would all be severed and broken in pieces before his triumphant march.

Not only so, but treasures of gold and silver buried under ground—the wealth of many nations, collected and stored in this vast and wealthy community of Babylon—would all come to Cyrus. The Lord seems to pay good wages for doing His work, and Cyrus was going to be much wealthier because he did the work of God, and when it was all accomplished he honestly acknowledged that God had done it: "The Lord God of heaven hath given me all the kingdoms of the earth; and he hath charged me to build him a house at Jerusalem, which is in Judah" (Ezra 1:2).

What Cyrus aimed at in his victories we may well guess, but we are not left in any doubt of God's purpose, for it is given in the second part of Isaiah 45:3—that Cyrus might come to know that the Lord is God, "that I, the Lord, which call thee by thy name, am the God of Israel." Furthermore in verse 4, He says that Israel would be released, and that in the day of great victory Cyrus might know that all he had been doing was fulfilling the purpose of God. This, therefore, was God's objective in using this man.

Here, then, is just a very brief glimpse of the hand of God that moves the world, of the things that were going on behind the scenes and the purposes of them in the mind of our sovereign Lord, to whom the nations of the earth are as a drop in the bucket, who one day will set His King upon His holy hill of Zion and give Him the heathen for His inheritance, and the uttermost parts of the earth for His possession.

Read again the amazing words in Matthew 25:31–34. Ask that you may have a Spirit-anointed mind to see the maze and confusion of all current events from the standpoint of the throne in heaven. Our God is on the throne. No human dictator, however powerful he may seem, can lift a little finger without permission from our risen, victorious, coming Saviour. He will raise up one, and put down another, that His purposes of redemption for His people may be brought to a wonderful and triumphant conclusion.

The words of this text, however, have a much more intimate and personal application, which will be more meaningful as you consider them against the background of what I have just been saying.

"I will give thee the treasures of darkness . . ." (Isaiah 45:3).

I don't want you to listen to these words as spoken to a heathen monarch, but as spoken by the Spirit of God to your own heart.

Do you think darkness has any treasures? Isn't darkness something of which we are all afraid? You remember the words of the Lord Jesus, "Men loved darkness rather than light, because their deeds were evil" (John 3:19). Darkness: the physical darkness of suffering, the agony of mental darkness, the spiritual darkness caused by a cloud between ourselves and God. Don't you think that these are things to be avoided at any cost? Surely, and yet the verse says, "I will give thee the *treasures* of darkness. . . ."

I want to speak about some of the treasures I have found, as a Christian, in days of darkness. First I would say that it takes darkness to put a man in his right perspective. How much the darkness reveals! Maybe you had not thought about that. It only reveals a little bit less than the light. Have you ever asked yourself what a strange world it would be if it consisted of twenty-four hours of daylight, and if the sun shone all the time? If it were like that, we would assume that this little earth is all that there is of God's universe, with a great fiery glow above giving us heat and light. How ignorant we would be of the vastness of God's creation, and of our real position in the universe!

But how much more fully do I understand the glory and power of the mind of the Lord when darkness falls! It is then I know how small I am.

When the Lord dropped the mantle of darkness in David's time he said, "When I consider thy heavens, the work of thy fingers, the moon and the stars, which thou hast ordained; What is man, that thou art mindful of him? and the son of man, that thou visitest him?" (Psalm 8:3, 4). It was the glory of something David had been unable to see until night fell that taught him most about God and about himself. "How great Thou art!" he cries, "and how insignificant I am!" It is darkness that puts man in his right perspective.

Further, it is darkness that pierces the mystery of suffering and pain. Darkness has great healing power. I am not a botanist as some of you may be, but I believe I am right in saying that there are some kinds of trees which, when they are planted on streets which are lit all through the night, do not grow. They suffer from a kind of insomnia that trees can have! When the sun goes down and the lights go up, they are never in the dark. They languish and become exhausted, being constantly in a blaze of light from which there is no relief or rest, so they have to stay awake.

Darkness is not merely negative—the absence of light—but a positive source of growth and personal enrichment. Therefore the psalmist could say, "Before I was afflicted I went astray: but now have I kept thy word. . . . It is good for me that I have been afflicted; that I might learn thy statutes" (Psalm 119:67, 71).

What a tremendous amount of light is shed by the treasures of darkness upon some baffling, mysterious experience, against which one has fought and said, "I must avoid this at any cost, and it must stop!"

Darkness also prepares me for my home in heaven. It was out of that strange, awful darkness from midday until three in the afternoon on the cross of Calvary that our Lord was made sin for us, when God, even the Father, turned His face away from His Son as He identified Himself with the sin of mankind. It was out of such deep darkness that heaven opened its gates wide to every believing heart.

Oh, how could you or I ever begin to value the treasure that comes out of that darkness? Every gift of God, every blessing of His Spirit, everything we have in Jesus Christ, find their source in the darkness of Calvary. "God, who commanded the light to shine out of darkness, hath shined in our hearts, to give the light of the knowledge of the glory of God in the face of Jesus Christ" (2 Corinthians 4:6).

Is God taking you today through dark experiences or some deep sorrow of heart? Is it the absence of any sense of His presence in your life at all, even though you have been a Christian for years, that makes it seem so dark today? Is it personal bereavement, even though perhaps that loss happened some years ago, but has left you so utterly alone? Is it discouragement? Is it perhaps misunderstanding and misrepresentation by other people, and especially by Christians? Is it that your service for the Master seems so fruitless, and you have not seen much blessing—if any—lately? Is it a problem in your life to which there seems no answer? Is it pain from which there seems no release at all, or circumstances from which there is no escape? Is there temptation which is so relentless that there is no relief from the pressure of it? Whatever it is, you feel so much in the dark today, and perhaps are asking why God does that to you.

I would make this suggestion because there are things that are precious to me that I have not read in a textbook, but which I have proved in the years of my life. I think God puts us into the darkness in order that we might possess the hidden riches of the secret places. I think He has been obliged to do it that we might, as it were, see the stars, and observe His greatness and our smallness. As Moses said on behalf of the Lord before the people entered into the land: "Thou shalt remember all the way which the Lord thy God led thee these forty years in the wilderness, to humble thee, and to prove thee, to know what was in thine heart, whether thou wouldest keep his commandments, or no" (Deuteronomy 8:2). This is repeated in the words of Job when he says, "I have heard of thee by the hearing of the ear: but now mine eye seeth thee. Wherefore I abhor myself, and repent in dust and ashes" (Job 42:5, 6).

I wonder if He needed darkness (and I can bear humble testimony to this) to humble us. Do you ever get resentful with people scandal mongering with their tongues about you, and you know all the time it isn't true? I used to get mad! I don't now, by the grace of God. He put me into a dark place to teach me how small and insignificant I am, and how great He is.

It is lovely to leave your cause with Jesus, and let Him work it out. But when you react and become resentful, God has to put you in the dark to show you that you are not really important at all. He has to teach you that the very circumstances and people whom you resent, and from whom you try to run away, are the very nails which the Lord is using to crucify the flesh.

Yes, darkness humbles us.

Now let me share something else. If you have been going through the darkness lately, perhaps it has been to stop your wandering and going astray, and to make you say with a full heart and with tears in your eyes,

> I've wandered far away from God,
> Now I'm coming home;
> The paths of sin too long I've trod,
> Lord, I'm coming home.

Did it take the darkness to make you afraid? Perhaps it did, and now you have begun nestling into the heart of God instead of wrestling. The light has been fierce, the glare of publicity unbearable, but God put you in the dark, for "the secret of the Lord is with them that fear him" (Psalm 25:14).

Did it take the darkness to stop you wandering and sinning, and to press you close to the heart of Jesus? I wonder.

Perhaps He has sent the darkness, as Isaiah writes (45:3), "that thou mayest know that I, the Lord, which call thee by thy name, am the God of Israel." Oh, the treasures of the secret place of communion with Jesus Christ! What a thrill it is if you happen to travel in another, foreign country, and maybe you are in a crowd with people you don't know all around you, and suddenly from somewhere in that crowd your name is called, and you find you have met an old friend in an unexpected place! That person perhaps was only a casual acquaintance, but if you were not too careful about the bounds of propriety, you would feel like hugging him! You felt so far away from home, and then you met someone whom you knew.

"I will give thee the . . . hidden riches of secret places . . ." (v. 3). It has taken darkness in my soul many times to take me into an intimate fellowship with the Lord who calls His own sheep by name and leads them out.

I hope I do not surprise or shock you, but I would never seek to preach above my own experience, and I would tell you no more than the truth when I say that if I only prayed when I felt like it, I would not do much praying. But it is darkness that has driven me into a deep fellowship with the Lord Jesus to discover some of the riches of secret places.

The wisest of all men (apart, of course, from the Lord Jesus who is unique and in a class all by Himself), Solomon, once said, "It is the glory of God to conceal a thing: but the honour of kings is to search out a matter" (Proverbs 25:2).

The glory of a king is not his little power, nor his little palace, nor his automobiles, but his ability to search out something. That is the glory of every king and priest unto God, the glory of your life and mine.

Do you remember the day when your children could not look above the level of the table, and had to stand on tiptoe to see what was going on? Then they got to a stage, in another month or two, when you could not leave them doing that. If you did, the ice-cream would go, other things would disappear as they learned to peek over the table and reach out for what they could see. Did you notice when your little child began to grow like that, he or she was always searching out different levels for different experiences? This is life; we are all doing that, even now, for it is the honor of a king to search out a matter.

Once I had a faith in the Lord Jesus which was little more than a lighthearted statement of doctrine which was perfectly sound; but my faith is not that now. It took darkness to make my faith real, to bring all that I believe in doctrine to be part of my very life and my very being. Do you see what I mean? I wonder if it has taken darkness to make your faith your very own?

A Christian home is a great blessing, but I am sure that the children of Christian parents are in great peril of a secondhand faith. Very often God has to put such dear folk—and how we would love to spare them from it!—in darkness until their faith becomes real. Don't despair, dear mother and father, of that boy or girl who at this time may seem to be at the other end of the earth, miles away from God—don't despair of them. You cannot talk to them about Jesus, but you can talk to Jesus about them. You cannot argue with them about Christ; you would waste your time. The moment you talk with them they answer back, and you feel so helpless and bereft. You cannot but grieve that the boy or girl for whom you spent so much and cared for so deeply could be in that position today. But remember, it takes darkness—night—to make their faith their own. A superficial credal statement is not enough, and there comes a day when, in brokenness of heart and spirit, they discover that you are right and they were wrong. God grant that that may be true of any dear child of yours today who seems far away from Him. It took darkness to do that for me.

In the early church, the believers built their doctrine on their experience. Their doctrine was required to explain their experience.

Now we have our doctrine, but we do not have much experience, and so we try to build an experience on doctrine.

There was a day when our Lord spoke about the man who had treasure hidden in a field, and what joy and wealth were his when it was discovered! I often wish the Lord had told us how he found it. I think it was probably when his hand was on the plough in the heat of the day, as he was digging some lonely furrow, ploughing and working, and suddenly he hit upon the treasure in a time of stress and weariness. What joy was his!

The Lord says in Psalm 18:11, "He made darkness . . . his pavilion. . . ." There are still times in my life when God puts me through experiences like this. I used to be afraid of them. There are times when He seems to take me into the dark, and I find myself saying, "Now, Lord, what are You going to show me in this experience?" I discovered that when you look at the dark clouds from the outside they are so black, and the experience is so fearful. But when you get right in the middle, it is as bright as the noonday sun. He makes the darkness His pavilion. He is right there in it to reveal something more of Himself.

You never can have a Safety-First campaign in the life of faith. In the adventure of a soul with God there is no such thing as that. You discover God in Jesus Christ, and He takes you on

by one step of faith after another, in the dark. Yet He promises
that "he that followeth me shall not walk in darkness, but shall
have the light of life" (John 8:12).

If God has been putting you through days and months, and
even years, of darkness, I do pray that you may be discovering
secret riches in secret places, and laying hold of the treasures
of darkness that come to you as you live in communion with the
living Lord Jesus.

> In heavenly love abiding,
> No change my heart shall fear;
> And safe is such confiding,
> For nothing changes here.
>
> The storm may roar without me,
> My heart may low be laid,
> But God is round about me,
> And can I be dismayed?
>
> Green pastures are before me,
> Which yet I have not seen;
> Bright skies will soon be o'er me,
> Where darkest clouds have been.
>
> My hope I cannot measure,
> My path to life is free;
> My Saviour has my treasure,
> And He will walk with me.
>
> ANNA L. WARING

10

Isaiah 45:5–19

Battling with God

Woe unto him that striveth with his Maker! Let the potsherd strive with the potsherds of the earth. Shall the clay say to him that fashioneth it, What makest thou? or thy work, He hath no hands? (Isaiah 45:9)

This is the answer of heaven to a man who is contending with God. To catch the full import of that verse, I would remind you of the context. Isaiah, under the inspiration of the Spirit of God, is speaking of a day when a heathen king would be used as an instrument of God to deliver His people from captivity and slavery in Babylon. But the Lord issues to Cyrus a solemn warning that, though he would indeed gain a notable victory, yet he is in His hand, whose dominion and sovereignty are absolute.

Notice the language of verses 5–7: what dramatic claims are made here! "I am the Lord, and there is none else, there is no God beside me: . . . I am the Lord, and there is none else. I form the light, and create darkness: I make peace, and create evil: I the Lord do all these things."

Here the Lord is speaking to a man whom He is going to use, and He reminds him that He is God alone, and there is no other God beside Him. If everyone in the world believed that today, there would be no idolatry at all. He is the only self-existent, eternal, infinite God, and all others who set themselves up in competition with Him are mere counterfeit. In verse 6 we are told that from the rising of the sun (that is, in the east) right through to the west, throughout the entire globe which we inhabit, He is Lord of all. Nothing is done without Him.

He forms the light—everything that is good and pleasant.

He creates darkness—all that is sinister and unpleasant.

He makes peace—all that is good.

He creates evil—not the evil of sin, for He is not the author of sin; but He creates the evil of punishment.

He is Lord of all.

So, therefore, in all the different events which befall us—light or darkness, sorrow or joy—there is a God who is the first cause of every one of them. This sovereign Lord, the all-wise God, makes provision for our comforts as well as the ordering of our crosses.

Now it is against the background of this tremendous claim of absolute dominion that we have the language of our text. He is the Maker of all things, therefore He is our Maker, and because He is this we must never contend, argue, or battle with Him. Nobody, says Isaiah, who hardens his heart will prosper. It is as absurd for a man to contend with God as it is for a piece of clay to find fault with the potter, asking why he made it in this shape and not in that; and even perhaps for that piece of clay to rise up and say when it is in the potter's hand, "You are so clumsy you are all thumbs—you work as if you haven't any hands at all!"

The question is, therefore, shall I contend with God, the One who has given me breath? Shall I doubt His power and challenge Him? Shall I say that my God has no hands, when His hands made me, and in those hands my life, my very breath, is even today?

To answer that question satisfactorily I would use Isaiah's illustration, and take you in your imagination to a potter's house where this almost frightening doctrine of the sovereignty of God is seen in a somewhat different light. It is interesting to note how often the Bible uses the illustration of the potter and the clay, always in the same connection. Isaiah uses it here, and it is to be found in Jeremiah 18, Zechariah 11, while Paul uses it in Romans 9. In every case it is given as an explanation of the sovereignty of God.

Come with me, therefore, into the potter's house, and what do you see when you get inside? First there is the potter, an intelligent, capable being. Then there is the wheel, an instrument by which he is going to accomplish his purposes with the clay. And you also see a mass of shapeless clay. It is not steel you see, but clay, a material that is pliable, the sort of stuff that is capable of responding to the mind of the potter. So in these things you see a perfect illustration of God's relationship to each of us today.

There is a Master Workman who has a thought in His mind, a passion in His heart, for your life and mine. Only He knows that thought.

Then there is yourself, the clay, capable of responding to the pressures that are put upon it by the wheel in the hand of the potter.

Then there is the turning of the wheels of circumstance, turning so swiftly sometimes that they frighten us, until one day they are set aside by the Potter when the work is done, and the clay is fashioned.

These are the things that are seen in the potter's house.

What has that picture to say to us in the light of our text? First, there is a principle taught here, on which I have already commented, of the absolute, total, complete sovereignty of God, and the necessity for my submission to it without question. The potter has a right which is absolute over the clay, and the clay cannot resist his hand. It has no right to suggest what form it should take.

We hear a lot these days about the *rights* of people. This passage of Scripture—and indeed the whole Bible—has to do with the *rights* of God. The truth is that no man has any right to complain whatever God may do with him. We know that our God is not willing that any should perish and yet, let us face this fact, He has the right to take the whole world and annihilate it. He has the right to sweep out of existence the entire human race who has thrown over His law and rejected the Christ of Calvary. That is God's perfect right.

If there is one doctrine that is more terrible to my mind than the sovereignty of God, it is the doctrine of the supremacy of man. If you and I, like Israel, seek to exercise power over the Almighty and contend, argue, resist Him, then ultimately we meet only disaster.

It is one thing, however, to hold the doctrine of the supremacy of God, but it is quite another thing to give Him the place in your life which that doctrine demands. To give Him His rightful place is to give Him the place of deity. Therefore the right of an individual in His presence is to have no desire, no claim, no wish, save only to discover the desire and the claim of God upon his life, and then to do it.

But you may say, "That piece of clay has no will. I have a will. It has no power to choose, but I do."

Oh, yes, certainly God gave you a will in order that you might choose your Master, and in choosing Him, choose your destiny. Our wills are not our own that we might make them His, and even as you choose your Master, you do so under the government of God from which there is no ultimate escape whatsoever. To submit to the will of God is to submit to the way of righteousness and peace. To choose another master is to spell the judgment of God upon a rebellious life. It is impossible to escape the judgment and the sovereignty of God.

If the potter had a right to complete authority over the clay, how much more has the eternal God an absolute authority over the will of man! The potter and the clay are two finite things. God is infinite, while you and I are finite. How much bigger is the margin between the infinite will of God and your life than between that of the potter and the clay! Therefore I repeat, if the potter has a right over the clay, how much more has God a right over you. The only path of wisdom is the path of uncompromising surrender to God, and that is the principle that is taught here. This is the lesson God was teaching Cyrus. He is saying the same thing to anyone who would begin to contend with his Maker.

If, however, you take the doctrine of the sovereignty of God like that, alone and exclusively, you find it the most terrifying thing in life—even repulsive. Too often we who preach the

Word preach submission to the sovereignty of God without any reference to the character of God. I shall never, as an individual, submit to the principle of that sovereignty without first coming to know something of His character. I will not submit, even though I am frail and weak, unless I see Him and know Him, and in a measure come to understand Him. Apart from that, I will begin to contend with Him in the language of Isaiah 45:9, "What makest thou? . . ." What hast thou brought forth? You handle me so clumsily that I think You have no hands at all!

God does not leave us like this. There is a purpose explained in the potter's house which makes me not want to run from His sovereignty, but rather makes me long to experience it more and more in my life.

Come with me again in your imagination to the potter's house, and what is he doing? Before he puts his hand upon the lifeless mass of clay he has a thought in his mind which will regulate all he is about to do. I watch him beginning his work. I cannot see what his purpose is, but he has a thought in his mind for that particular piece of clay, of which the clay is ignorant. However, because of its nature, the clay is capable of revealing the thought which is in the mind of the potter, and of expressing it simply by submission to the potter's hand.

Before God ever made you, He had a plan for your life. He who is so careful even for the grass in the field which is there today and tomorrow is cast into the oven, who is so concerned about the most insignificant things, He has a plan for you and for me. To Jeremiah He said, "Before I formed thee . . . I knew thee" (Jeremiah 1:5). Because God has a plan for your life, it determines where you are born, the country you live in, the place where you work, how you come into the world, and many more things, for God has a thought in His mind before anybody else thought about you.

I see this sovereignty expressed not only as a plan in His mind, but in the pressure of His hand on the clay. Watch the potter at work. He is seated at a wheel underneath which are treadles that he moves with his feet to regulate its pace—to slow it down and to speed it up. On the wheel there is a piece of clay.

Presently the wheel begins to turn, and as it does, the potter's hands move and press upon the clay. They give a little here, and press a little harder there, in order to bring the thought that is in his mind for the clay into reality. The two most important factors are the pressure of his hand and the speed of the wheel, and he controls both of them. It is he who applies the pressure. It is he who regulates the speed.

The plan that was in God's mind for you is brought into reality in exactly the same way. There are the same two deciding factors: first the pressure of His hand, and secondly the pace of the wheel.

Sometimes through a message from the pulpit, or through personal study of the Word of God, sometimes by the action of conscience you become conscious of the pressure of His hand. Perhaps you have said, as I have, "How I have felt the hand of God upon me today!"

The pace of the wheel is indicated by the way the Lord arranges your circumstances, moving them at such a pace and in such a direction that they enable Him to form a shapeless piece of clay into a vessel of His choice. "And we know that all things work together for good to them that love God, to them who are the called according to his purpose" (Romans 8:28). Yes! Providence is the handmaid of God's grace. The two are allies. The God of redemption is the God of circumstance.

Are you feeling the pressure of God's hand and the pace of the wheel? When the pressure is greatest and the speed is fastest, I believe it is because He has in mind the production of a very special kind of vessel. When He fashioned Moses, Joseph, David and Daniel, Peter and Paul, how the wheel turned!

Think about Joseph and the turn of the wheel in his life—its revolving almost makes me giddy to think about it! A sheltered home, and the wheel turns; a pit, and the wheel turns; a slave market, the wheel turns again; Potiphar's house with its luxury and temptation, and the wheel turns; a prison cell, the wheel turns again; the palace and ultimately his elevation to be second in the land with Pharaoh. How the wheel turned in Joseph's life!

Yet not one inch did it move without the hand of the Master Potter being on the clay. God was making a special vessel.

Maybe that is why the pressure of His hand upon your life is almost terrifying, and the speed of the wheel seems so fast. God's sovereignty is being expressed by a plan in His mind which is being brought into action by the pressure of His hand and the speed of the wheel.

His sovereignty is also expressed by the passion in His heart for you. In the potter's house again I watch him with his hand upon the clay. What is his passion for that clay? I will tell you: perfection, nothing less. When the job is done and the wheel has stopped revolving, the clay will come out of his hand and he will see that he has turned out a work that is absolutely without flaw. His name and reputation are at stake in doing that, so not a single error must be in the clay when it is complete.

How that lights up to my heart the apparent mystery of the insistence of the Potter in breaking up every hard lump of clay that He meets! He will break it apart as He puts the pressure on. He will keep the speed of the wheel going until that hard lump of clay gives in and breaks in His hand, and so He can form it as He wants it to be. It isn't because He is a hard Master, but He is more concerned with our perfection than our comfort!

Now that is the ruling passion in the heart of God for everyone of us, that we might be conformed to the image of His Son. It is the passion for character and holiness. It is the longing that we might bear the image of Jesus, who was the express image of His Person, says the writer to the Hebrews. God's passion for the shapeless bit of clay—you and me—is that we are to be like Him, therefore He does not consider our comfort. The ultimate goal is so much more important. That is why some of us are ill at ease sometimes in church and after it, and why some get mad with the preacher!

I ask you very seriously to consider whether it is not the preacher with whom you are angry, but with the pressure of the hand of God. That is why you have sleepless nights and miserable days: the wheel has turned and the hand has continued to press upon you. It is your sovereign Lord wanting His rightful place in your life, the place of deity. He will be satisfied with nothing less. The thought of sovereignty may frighten you, for it sounds like tyranny, demanding submission, and you are afraid of that. Remember that the One who demands it does so in love.

We have seen a principle taught here: His absolute right because of His sovereignty. The purpose in His hand and in His mind is shown, but it is all terrifying until a Person is revealed. Who is the Potter? There need be no argument about this, for the Potter is God. But who is God? God is love. I could say a lot more about Him than that. There are many other attributes, but they are all summed up in these words, God is love. I am not afraid of submitting to love, and as He presses and breaks my life in His hand, it is only that He might remake it. If He crushes, it is only that He might re-create.

If you look closely at the hands of the heavenly Potter you will see that each one has a hole in it, for those hands have been pierced with nails as He hung upon a cross. If you would know the truth concerning the principle of His sovereignty and the purpose of it, you must lie down in the heart of God. What do I mean by this? Two things: first that we have to exercise faith in the plan of the Potter. I accept it as best for me because it is His plan. How elementary that is, but how difficult to believe! Yes, every turn of the wheel, every pressure of the hand, is really for the best. He asks for implicit faith that through every turn and every pressure He will shape a vessel that shall be for His glory. Until I accept that, I battle with God, and imply that I know better than He.

Will you yield today to the pressure of His hand? There is only one point at which the Potter hurts the clay, and that is where the resistance of the clay is complete. Oh, how great is the pressure at the point of resistance! God is in control of your circumstances; He has you in His hand, and at the place where you deny and defy Him, there everything is against you, and all goes wrong. The world and God are against you because at that point you are putting on resistance, so that you can say with

David, "Thy hand was heavy upon me: my moisture is turned into the drought of summer" (Psalm 32:4), because you resisted the hand of the Potter.

You must have faith to accept His plan, but also you must delight in the passion of His heart for you. You must share His longing for His character to be revealed in you, and His great desire for you to reflect His glory.

Answer this question to the Potter in whose hand you are: is that your chief concern? How much time have you given this week telling Him that you desire above all else that you might share His glory and His concern for your life? Is your cry, "Oh God, for Jesus' sake, glorify Yourself in this bit of clay"?

That is His passion. It is not merely a passive surrender, but your whole heart, soul, and being is concerned to "work out your own salvation with fear and trembling. For it is God which worketh in you both to will and to do of his good pleasure" (Philippians 2:12, 13). As a matter of fact, He is calling you to fellowship with Himself in perfecting this clay; and surely that is an evidence of your regeneration. It is an indication of your new birth that you share the heart of God in His passion and concern for yourself.

It is a wonderful thing when a little child looks up into the face of his parents and says, "If you say so, it must be best." What a joy it is to be trusted! Have you ever given God the joy of knowing that you trust Him? Have you ever shared the pleasure and the thrill of His heart as you have said, "Lord, have Thine own way; Thou art the Potter, I am the clay"? God grant that you might stay that rebellion, and stop battling with Him. The pressure is from a crucified hand, and the mind that guides the hand and the pace of the wheel is the mind that planned your salvation. When you rebel you take the clay out of His hands, and that spells ruin.

Probably you have never seen a potter's field, but what wrecks one sees there! Bits of clay here and there, all thrown aside useless.

Charge me with fanciful interpretation of Scripture if you will, but the potter's field is last mentioned in Scripture in very strange company. Matthew 27:7, 8 tells us that the priests bought the potter's field with the price of Him whom they pierced, and they called it the "field of blood."

Are you saying, "Oh, I'm no use to God! He has cast me off, and I'm hopeless, spoiled! He had me in His hand, but I rebelled against His will and became broken. Now I have just been cast aside among the wrecks in the potter's field."

Ah, but that field was purchased with blood, the blood of Jesus Christ.

We are told that when the "clay was marred in the hand of the potter: so he made it again another vessel, as seemed good to the potter to make it" (Jeremiah 18:4).

Blessed be God! He came to the potter's field, took the wrecks in His hand to make them again into useful things as He saw fit, and as they submitted to His pressure. By the mystery of His being sold for the price of a slave, He has bought the field so that wrecks can be remade, if they yield to His plan.

You may say that we have wandered a long way from Cyrus, king of Persia, and from Isaiah 45:9. Well, if so, I hope that I have wandered so far that I have entered right into your heart! I want you to see behind the principles of sovereignty the purpose of it, and to know that God's purpose is best. If that frightens you, behind the purpose is a Person whose hands have been nailed to the cross. May you come to understand as never before the reason for the absolute authority and dominion of God in your life, and to see that behind it He has a purpose which He brings to pass with the turning of the wheel and the pressure of His hand upon the clay of your life and character.

11

Isaiah 45:20–25

Where To Look for Life

*Look unto me, and be ye saved, all the ends of the earth:
for I am God, and there is none else.* (Isaiah 45:22)

On Sunday, January 6, 1850, a young lad not quite sixteen
years of age was walking through a village street in a little town
some fifty miles from London, England. It was a bitterly cold
day and the snow was falling heavily. He was anxious to find the
house of God, deeply conscious of his need of Him, and of the
breakdown, sin, and failure of his life even at that young age.
As he made his way through the street with the snow falling, he
felt it was too far to go to the church which he had intended to
visit, so he walked down a back lane and entered a little Metho-
dist chapel. He sat down on a seat near the back, and it was as
cold inside as it was out! The congregation mustered about
thirteen people.

Five minutes after the service was due to begin at eleven
o'clock, the preacher announced for the morning had not made
his appearance. He had been delayed by the weather. So one
of the deacons came to the rescue and began conducting the
service, and after a little while he announced his text: "Look
unto me, and be ye saved, all the ends of the earth: for I am God,
and there is none else."

After ten minutes he had said all he knew about his text, and
the service was terminating when suddenly the deacon, notic-
ing the miserable looking young man at the back of the church,

131

said to him aloud in the presence of the thirteen other people, "Young man, you look very miserable this morning. You need to look to Jesus and be saved. Young man, look, look to Jesus."

Somehow in a very strange and amazing way that young man looked from the depths of his soul into the very heart of God. He went out from that church, and he tells that as he walked through the streets, his burden had been lifted, never to return again. He walked with a new spring in his step, a new joy in his face, a new sense of peace in his heart. He had looked and lived. That young man, as many of you probably know, was Charles Haddon Spurgeon, who for another forty-three years lived to become one of the greatest preachers of his generation. And it all began when, as a young fellow scarcely sixteen years of age, he looked and lived.

Perhaps you have lived for quite a while with the atmosphere of religion and Christianity, but you have never really looked to the Lord Jesus in a way that transforms life. If you did at one time look, maybe somehow your eyes have been taken away from the Saviour, and now you are burdened with a sense of deep need and the consciousness that you are far from God though you may be, geographically, within the area of Christian things. It is my privilege and responsibility to ask you to turn your heart to the One in whom you may find life.

I want you to notice the repetition of a phrase which occurs in the portion of God's Word under consideration. When the Holy Spirit repeats Himself it is well for us to give attention, for this is what He wishes to stress, and upon which we must concentrate our thinking.

Isaiah 45:5 says, "I am the Lord, and there is none else, there is no God beside me." The end of verse 6 reads, "I am the Lord, and there is none else. . . ." The last words of verse 14, "and there is none else, there is no God." Similarly in verse 18, "I am the Lord, and there is none else." In verse 21, "there is no God else beside me; a just God and a Saviour; there is none beside me." In verse 22, "I am God, and there is none else."

Let us take a flight of imagination and picture a time when this universe, as we know it, was not in existence, when there were no stars, no sun or moon, no heavens or earth. But there was God, who is from everlasting to everlasting; He had no beginning and will have no ending. At this time the earth, so to speak, was slumbering. It was there in embryo. But God was there in a vast canopy of space with no universe, no stars, no people to worship or love Him. The only light in all that immense emptiness was the glory of His countenance—God, the great, holy, majestic, omnipotent, with no beginning or ending —God.

"In the beginning God created the heaven and the earth" (Genesis 1:1).

There came a moment when the mind of God began to put into action that which had always been slumbering in His heart. There came the sun, the moon and stars, a universe—a little part of which we call the earth. On that planet Earth, He put a man made in His own image.

As you contemplate God in that connection, immediately you will recognize that anything created would be insignificant compared with the Creator. How small even the universe is compared with the great, mighty God! Therefore, because that is so, how impudent of anything or anyone whom God made ever to imagine that he could set himself against the Creator. But that is what Satan did. That is what the inhabitants of this little Earth of ours have done. Creatures of time that exist for some seventy years, more or less, have set themselves up in rivalry to the eternal God, the One who is without beginning or ending.

Ever since then, it has been the great purpose of God all through history to teach mankind that there is no God beside Him; there is none else. Especially is this true concerning the greatest work that God has ever done, and that is the saving of a soul from himself and his sin.

Before we consider this aspect, let us think of the ways in which the Lord has sought through the ages to demonstrate in different ways to different people that there is no God beside Him.

He sought to teach that truth concerning the idols of heathen nations, and you might well ask where are the idols of ancient empires today. The gods before whom a great proportion of the world used to worship are no longer in existence, because the Lord showed great empires, through His prophets and people, that there was no God beside Him.

A visit to the Middle East will reveal the ruins of ancient Greece, Babylon, Rome, these great and mighty empires which at one time seemed to be omnipotent. Now they are buried beneath ruins, a testimony to the truth of our text, that beside our God there is none other.

He not only sought to teach empires, but the kings who ruled over them. Remember, for instance, Nebuchadnezzar as he walked through Babylon and said, "Is not this great Babylon, that I have built. . . ?" (Daniel 4:30). A man, a king, did I say? See him later crawling on all fours, with his hair like eagle's feathers, his fingernails like the claws of a bird (v. 33). Yes, a man who set himself against God whom He humbled, and to whom He said, "There is no God beside me."

Belshazzar, in Daniel 5, drank out of the sacred vessels of the temple, setting himself up as the king of all the earth, one day saw the writing on the wall, and before he knew what was happening, was dead.

In the New Testament recall a man named Herod of whom, when the people heard him speak, they said, ". . . It is the voice of a god, and not of a man" (Acts 12:22). But he was eaten of worms and died (v. 23).

So through history one finds men like Alexander and Napoleon, and nearer in time, Hitler and Stalin, before whom God stands and says, "Beside me there is no God."

The hardest place where God has to speak that Word is to His own children, redeemed by His blood, who find it so hard to believe that there is no other God beside Him. That was true of those in the church (if I may use the word) of the Old Testament, who because of their disobedience were sent into captivity in Babylon. It has been true through all history that the church has found it desperately difficult to acknowledge that the Christ of Calvary, of resurrection power and of coming glory, is King of kings and Lord of lords, and that there is no God beside Him.

Many a child of God has had days of ease and prosperity when things have gone well, but alas, the Christian finds himself worshiping the god of materialism. Wealth and riches, comfort and enjoyment, now come first in his life, and God has to strike him low. Through chastening and affliction, often through sorrow and trouble—through any experience—God has to teach him the lesson that there is no God beside Him. Ah yes, it is hard for the child of God really to believe that.

It would seem that no man gets very far in Christian living until he has come to say with the Apostle Paul, "Unto me, who am less than the least of all saints, is this grace given, that I should preach . . . the unsearchable riches of Christ" (Ephesians 3:8).

It is amazing, when you think about it, in the conception of who God is, that all through history He has been seeking to teach His people that beside Him there is no God. That is the emphasis of these verses in Isaiah 45, a demonstration of the fact that there is no rival to our God.

As I said earlier, this is especially true in the greatest thing that God has ever done, namely, the salvation of a soul. By the same token, the hardest thing for a man ever to do—as he seeks to grope his way through intellectual fog, misunderstanding, and theological argument, in his search after God—is to come to a place where he is honestly prepared to say that beside the Lord there is none else.

The text suggests this in three different ways: God speaks to an individual in order to show him that there is no God beside Him when He says, "Look unto me. . . ." So first we are shown the Person to whom we are to look: "unto me." Then that which we are to do: to look; and there is nothing hard in this, it is basically simple, but in looking we are admitting that there is no other God beside Him. Forsaking all confidence in any other idol or god, for salvation we look to Him: "Look unto me, and be ye saved, all the ends of the earth: for [round the whole circle of the globe] . . . there is none else" (v. 22). Thirdly, the people who are to look: all the ends of the earth, for beside Him there is no God.

Perhaps you are quite surprised because, though you have been so long under the sound of the Word and in the circle of Christian things, yet if you once have looked at Christ, it was a long time ago, and you desperately need again to turn your eyes upon Jesus.

So let us concentrate our attention upon this Person upon whom we are to look. For this great work of salvation He says "Look unto me." Sometimes it is difficult to do that, and far easier to look at the church, or the preacher, or to some form of ritual and ceremony. Oh no, God says these will never save, for they cannot bring the blessing of His life and power.

We are to look away from all this to Him, the Lord Jesus, and where do we look? At a place called Calvary. Not necessarily to Bethlehem (though Bethlehem leads to Calvary), not primarily to the life that He lived as recorded in the gospels, because though that life paved the way to His death we are to look at the cross.

How long is it since you paused and thought about Him? Have you looked at Him lately, and seen His head crowned with thorns, and the blood caused by their piercing? Have you looked at His head bowed meekly upon His breast in absolute submission to the will of God?

Have you looked at His side that was torn with a spear, out of which flowed blood and water? Have you looked at His feet that were almost rent in two as they bore the weight of His body hanging upon the tree, and His hands that were nailed to the cross?

Have you ever really looked, and said: "Lord Jesus, You did all that for me!"

Have you looked at an empty tomb? Have you looked at Him, the great High Priest who ever lives to make intercession for us all? For ". . . if any man sin, we have an advocate with the Father, Jesus Christ the righteous" (1 John 2:1).

Have you looked and seen Him as the One before whom every knee shall bow, King of kings and Lord of lords?

This is what God asks us to do; this is what He expects of us. He who had no beginning and has no ending, who put the whole universe into action, who sent His Son that He might be the Saviour of the world—He says that we must look to Him. I wonder if you have.

"But," you may be saying, "for months I have been trying to see Him."

God does not say you are to see Him: He says you are to look. Therefore, have you looked to Jesus?

Look unto ME, is His Word, which means looking away from the church because that will save nobody; away from the preacher because he can disappoint and disillusion you; away from all outward form and ceremony. You must look off from all this clear to the throne and there, in your heart, see the risen, reigning Lord Jesus Christ.

That is where you are to look for life. But what must you do to obtain life? You are to look.

All through history people have wanted a very complicated religion, and many liked the demands made upon them by the priesthood. I honestly believe if I could guarantee that if anyone were to walk a thousand miles on bare feet along a highway he would be absolutely sure of making it to heaven, there would be some people who would do it. They would feel, by doing so, that they had done something meritorious and worthy which had earned them a reward. I fear we like religion to which we attach personal merit, but God calls us away from it by saying one simple thing, "LOOK!"

One can read many books on theology which expound all kinds of things in an attempt to show how man can reach God, but these theories can be far from the truth. The Holy Spirit needs exactly four letters, two of them the same, to tell us what to do: l-o-o-k. That is all. It is the simplest, basic thing any person can do, yet the most difficult to do in daily living. Man in his pride prefers his faith to be made complicated because this panders to his intellect. The Lord only asks for the thing that He knows is essential: the Creator asks of His creatures that they might look.

What does it mean to look? It is not what I see of myself that matters. It is not my calculation, my opinion, my ideas or conception of what I am, but my conception of what God in Jesus Christ is that matters. It is the objective look to Him that has saving power.

Maybe one of the most difficult things for any of us to do is to look away from ourselves, from within us, and look away to the Lord Jesus on Calvary, and now upon the throne.

Some people say, "I'm too bad," and others, "I'm too good," or "I'm all right as I am," or again, "I'm too sinful." Oh, that we would look away from ourselves, good or bad, and look right off to Jesus!

To look signifies the desire for God, the longing after Him, the heart-hunger to know Him. It is the deep burden of sin, the consciousness of failure and sinfulness. To look at Christ is to lean upon Him with all the strength of heart and soul. It is to cling on and trust in Him. Unless a man is totally and utterly resting upon and committed to the Christ of power and glory, life becomes a state of hopelessness.

Have you looked like that? That is how Charles Haddon Spurgeon was saved, and in just the same way you, too, may know His eternal salvation and blessing.

Who are the people who have to look? "Look unto me, and be ye saved, all the ends of the earth. . . ."

Often we interpret the word *salvation* in a very narrow sense. It is something much greater and vaster than we can imagine. It is far bigger than merely salvation in the forgiving of our sins, though of course that is basic for our acceptance by a holy God. It is salvation from racial prejudice, for one thing, from thinking that because a man's skin is a different color he is an inferior creature. One day there will be deliverance from all social evils of our race and of our world, because we read in Isaiah 45:23, ". . . unto me every knee shall bow, every tongue shall swear."

Salvation is so vast that it is not possible now to enter into the subject more fully. But to return to our question, who are the people who have to look? ". . . all the ends of the earth"—that

is overwhelming! It is the Word of omnipotence and authority.
Of course it means the heathen, those who today have never
heard about the Lord Jesus Christ. As I read that verse a fire is
kindled in my heart, a burden and concern make me ask myself,
"Why do I live as I do when millions today have never heard
about my Saviour?" It puts feet to my praying and sacrifice to
my giving, for ultimately nothing matters but that the ends of
the earth shall hear.

". . . the ends of the earth . . ." means that, but it also means
something else which I wish to bring home to your heart. Do
you think the phrase typifies something merely geographical?
Not a bit of it! I believe there is something very deep and
personal about it, because though geographically you are under
the sound of God's Word, yet spiritually you could be at the
ends of the earth in your distance from God.

I wonder if you have ever really looked at Him in a way that
will draw you near to Him as you experience His saving and
delivering power.

It could be, alas, that you know you are so far away from Him
that the distance is immeasurable. Your heart is cold and dry
and dead; your mind does not respond to the truth, and God is
millions of miles away. The ends of the earth, that is where you
are. There is no point in wondering why that is so, for many
reasons may have put you there—possibly rebellion or some
sad, tragic circumstance, which only you know about—but in
your heart and soul you are at the other end of the earth from
the Lord in heaven. Your church service may appear real, your
profession of faith sincere, but Jesus Christ is a tragic unreality
in your life.

Therefore His Word comes to you, I trust, with the authority
of the Holy Spirit, "Look unto me, and be ye saved, all the ends
of the earth. . . ."

"Look": the terms of salvation are the same for a man who is
spiritually miles away and the man of whom God can say, "Thou
art not far from the kingdom."

"Look": and the terms are the same for the man who is in the
upper-income bracket and the one who is in skid row. The

terms are the same for the man who is drinking himself to
death, and the man who is clothed with his robe of self-righteousness.

The terms are absolutely universal, and are the simple and
glorious truth that today a man can break through the mists of
his mind and intellect, the things that hide God from him, and
by His grace he can break through the tragedy of sin and breakdown and look to Jesus.

On one occasion I was staying in Edinburgh, Scotland. It was
cold and foggy, and as I looked out of my hotel window I could
not even see Edinburgh Castle, which stood just across the road.
It is no wonder the Scots call the city "Auld Reekie," for it just
reeked with smoke and dirt! But when I awakened the next
morning and drew the blind, the city was clothed in a robe of
spotless white, for overnight there had been six inches of snow.
I have rarely seen such a beautiful scene as I saw that morning.
The place which had been so dark and dirty, so smoky and
grimy, was completely transformed by a clean and spotless
mantle. Immediately, as I saw it, my heart went up to God, and
I thought, Oh, Lord, though my sins be as scarlet, they shall be
as white as snow; though they be red like crimson, they shall be
as wool!

What transformations His salvation can bring! Just look from
the depths of your heart to the throne of God. Abandon impurity and sin, religion and self-righteousness, and look right off
to the Lord Jesus Christ.

Look again at Calvary, and remember that His righteousness
and strength are ours, for the One whose blood was shed for our
redemption is the One before whom every knee shall bow, and
every tongue confess that He is Lord, to the glory of God the
Father.

12

Worship and Witness

*I bring near my righteousness; it shall not be far off, and
my salvation shall not tarry: and I will place salvation in
Zion for Israel my glory. (Isaiah 46:13)*

As you read this chapter, you will see that its story (recorded
about 170 years before the actual event) anticipates the day
when, in fulfillment of God's purpose which can never be
thwarted, Cyrus, king of Persia, would invade Babylon, and in
so doing would be instrumental in releasing God's people from
bondage.

In the opening verses of this chapter is the graphic picture of
the two Babylonian gods, Bel and Nebo—after whom the two
great kings were named, Belshazzar and Nebuchadnezzar—
being carried off in carts as trophies of the Persian victory. Of
course, the victors would have no place in their lives for the
worship of Babylon's idols, but their capture demonstrated the
completeness of victory, the folly of the people, and the futility
of the gods to rescue them from defeat. The sixth verse suggests
that they had been made at great expense and lavishly deco-
rated, yet these tawdry idols only emphasized in time of defeat
their futility, and the absolute stupidity of people for ever having lowered their dignity to worship them.

Now, of course, these details are past history, but the principles are up-to-date. I would underline a lesson now to say
that any nation which departs from her former glory and the

worship of the living God to the worship of idols, whatever form those idols may take—whether they be wooden images, or mighty men, or weighty armaments, or lust of power—whenever a nation looks to these things for deliverance in times of crisis, it finds them only a burden. Such a nation proves once again the absolute folly and futility of demeaning itself in departing from God to worship idols.

In his State of the Union message in 1962, the late President Kennedy said, "World order will be secured only when the whole world has laid down these weapons which seem to offer us present security but threaten the future survival of the human race. That armistice day seems very far away." How true! But if we are to put down those things in which we have put our confidence falsely, and forsake our dependence upon armaments and material strength, what are we going to put in their place? What is to be the ground of confidence if that in which we have trusted proves to be false? For no nation or individual can live in a vacuum.

Now this chapter has the tremendous answer to that question, for it paints in a vivid picture a threefold contrast between the idols of Babylon and Jehovah, the God of Israel and our God. This contrast goes far deeper and further than ancient heathendom. It comes right to where you and I live.

Whatever a person may put in the place of sovereignty which rightly belongs to the Lord who made him and bought him with His precious blood, he only erects an idol before which he worships and in which he places his faith. By so doing, he lowers the whole dignity of his manhood, and reaps the inevitable reward of the judgment of a holy God—a judgment, incidentally, which is not only reserved for a dreadful future day, but one of which God gives a man and a nation full warning in the course of life here on earth.

Look then at this contrast between Jehovah and every other idol, and let me ask you very earnestly to put yourself into this amazing picture.

In the first place there is a contrast in burden bearing. In

Isaiah 46:7 it is said of the idol, "They bear him upon the shoulder, they carry him. . . ." In other words, the idol is something which has to be carried until it becomes a crushing burden.

See now what the Lord says in verse 4: "And even to your old age I am he; and even to hoar hairs will I carry you: I have made, and I will bear; even I will carry, and will deliver you."

A man makes and then carries his idol! Many people spend their whole lifetime at the job: making that which in their own imagination is worthy of their worship! They make it and surround themselves with it, then they worship it, and spend their whole lives propping it up until it becomes a tremendous, crushing, overwhelming burden.

In glorious contrast God makes and offers to carry the man.

If you turn from the worship of God as revealed in Jesus Christ the Lord, immediately you make yourself an idol which, though it seems to offer present security, threatens your future survival. To some folk, even their religion is a burden—a burden of ritual and ceremony, a burden of duty and service. Others who yield themselves wholly to God find that religion in Jesus Christ, far from being something they carry, in fact carries them. That is exactly the intention of the Christian faith. It isn't something you carry as a dreadful load; it is designed to put a lever under the weight of your life and to carry you through. If your heart is right with God, if there is a living faith in Him, then your religion cannot be a burden, because He is the great burden bearer.

Primarily He bears the burden of our sin, the root cause of all the trouble. Isaiah 53:4, 5 says, "Surely he hath borne our griefs, and carried our sorrows: . . . But he was wounded for our transgressions, he was bruised for our iniquities. . . ."

Though this world is dark with sin, violence, and crime, He has borne it at the cross, and He will not rest until one day He comes again to put down all sin, to rule in righteousness, and to fill the world with His glory. He bears the burden of our sin, for He bore it all at Calvary—the crushing, intolerable load of the idol which we have worshiped.

Frankly, I don't believe there is any such person as an atheist. People almost pride themselves on such a philosophy as they boastfully say, "There is no God." This really means they worship themselves, they have their own god; because of the kind of creature man is, he is incapable of living without worshiping something. Perhaps the greatest form of conceit and idolatry is to worship oneself. But Jesus Christ even bears the burden of sinful independence when He took it to the cross, suffering under its guilt and weight, that He might lift the burden. What is more, having done that, bless His holy name, He bears the burden of our life work and responsibility, the task which often threatens to overwhelm us, the responsibilities which sometimes seem too heavy to bear and become a dead, crushing weight.

Once a person acknowledges his need and comes to Christ in repentance and faith, and experiences the burden of sin lifted, then He comes and places underneath the lever of His everlasting arms, and bears the burden of life.

There is an old but apt story of a man traveling along in an automobile who saw a poor fellow standing at the side of the road, carrying a large and heavy sack. He offered him a lift, and the man got in the car but kept the sack on his shoulder. The driver said, "Why don't you put your sack down?" The man replied, "Well, sir, I'm so grateful that you are carrying me I don't think it is fair to ask you to carry my sack as well!"

The Psalmist says, "Cast thy burden on the Lord, and he shall sustain thee" (Psalm 55:22). The Apostle Peter writes, "Casting all your care upon him; for he careth for you" (1 Peter 5:7).

I love that verse, for on August 10, 1926, in a little tavern near the boundary of the old Roman Empire in Northumberland, England, I cast my guilt and my burden at the feet of Jesus, and bless Him, He has carried me ever since, and will continue to do so right through until I get to heaven!

It is my responsibility to ask you, is your religious experience a burden that you are carrying, or have you found that the Lord Jesus Christ has begun to carry you?

Is there a heart that is willing to lay
Burdens on Jesus' breast?
He is so loving and gentle and true,
Come unto Him and be blest!

Note further the contrast in activity: "they . . . set him in his place, and he standeth; from his place shall he not remove . . ." (Isaiah 46:7). The prophet is speaking of the gods of Babylon who are completely immobile. What a graphic picture of the helpless condition of inactivity on the part of the idol, as it stands by watching the complete overthrow and destruction of a nation that has worshiped it! It has no suggestion to offer; it has no counsel to give; it has no remedy to suggest. Desperately the worshiper seeks its aid, but all in vain. There it stands, immobile and dumb.

Now notice the contrast in verse 13, "I bring near my righteousness. . . ." Here is the Lord making the move and taking the initiative. What a contrast! In the constant battle of life between men and God, we spend our time running away from Him while He is continually in pursuit with a love that will not let us go. Even though we may be (in the words of verse 12) ". . . far from righteousness," God brings near His own righteousness. Even though we may be clothed with all the filthy rags of our own wretchedness and failure, at that point He brings near His own, in order that He might cover all our filthiness with His spotlessness.

A certain night club in London had a very lurid reputation, and the story of its opening is quite extraordinary. A young fellow, who had been living a very wild life, came to the age of discretion and maturity when he was due to inherit from his father quite a fortune. He demanded the whole amount from his father, and informed him he was going to open the hottest night club in London, and his plan was "to paint the town red." The father was a godly man, and to hear his son talk like that broke his heart. However, plans were made, a site was purchased, and the night club was built.

Then came the great opening day which was well advertised in the press. As the young fellow went along to the opening, with all the swagger and pride of his accomplishment, when he reached the place he found to his amazement his father standing at the door. Already he had driven away a number of potential patrons, and he was continuing to do so as the people lined up to enter. The young man ran up to him, grabbed hold of him, and said in fury, "You get out of the way. This is my club, not yours."

The father looked at him straight between the eyes as he replied, "My son, no one will ever enter this building tonight except over my dead body."

People talk about hell and judgment, and think it is severe. But I declare to you in the name of our wonderful Lord Jesus, that no one will go into a Christless eternity except he who tramples underfoot the blood of Jesus Christ, and turns his back upon God's offer of salvation at Calvary. God's whole purpose of redemption is to separate man from the thing which He must judge; because He is holy, He is inevitably bound to condemn and destroy that which is sinful. His whole plea to every soul is that they might be separated from the sin that ensnares and drags them down. If they refuse Him, it is only logical that they must become involved in the judgment of the thing which He must condemn.

Such is the activity of God today, to bring near His righteousness as the answer to our deepest need, while every false god stands silent, the very silence mocking us that we have ever turned from the living Saviour to worship another. But He took the initiative when He stepped out of heaven and came down from glory to purchase our pardon at Calvary, and now He is offering us a righteousness that is perfect and complete, which we can receive as a free gift, or else we will never receive it at all.

There is not only a contrast in burden bearing and in activity, but there is also a contrast in power. ". . . one shall cry unto him, yet can he not answer, nor save him out of his trouble" (v. 7).

Worship that seemed sufficient in peaceful times had proved

totally inadequate when the crisis came. That was the lesson Babylon learned. Lip service to a god who was not real was absolutely useless when the chips were down.

Are we not proving that today? This world, involved as it is in a global civil war, presents a terrifying picture, and the gods in which we place our trust are in fact threatening our destruction. I wonder if we who profess to be Christians are reaping the fruit of years of lip service to the Lord who has never been real to us, while the true worship of our heart has been given elsewhere.

A statesman has said, "If we cannot fulfill our own ideals, we cannot expect other people to accept them." Of course not, and we have set up the ideal of a Christian society, but we do not attain to it because our God is not real. He is merely the Patron of the society instead of Lord of all. God is not here to be patronized; He is to be obeyed.

To illustrate this, please turn to Luke 8, the parable of the sower. The story is recorded in other gospels, but I refer to Luke's account because the wording is so striking. As the sower sowed his seed, "some fell upon a rock; and as soon as it was sprung up, it withered away, because it lacked moisture" (v. 6). By way of interpretation, our Lord said in verse 13, "They on the rock are they, which, when they hear, receive the word with joy; and these have no root, which for a while believe, and in time of temptation fall away."

I want these words to sound like an alarm bell in your soul: "have no root." Examine yourself in His presence, in the light of those words. Have you received the Word joyfully? Have your feelings been stirred time and time again? Have impressions been made? But to hear with the ears is one thing, to receive Christ into the depths of your being is another.

The strange paradox (maybe your experience will confirm what I say) is that very often the man who responds superficially so easily and quickly to the Word is the man who has the hardest heart. The seed fell on ground, says the Lord, with a rocky foundation, and when it began to take root it found downward growth was prevented by hard stones. The seed then began to spend its strength in pushing up green shoots as high as it could, but because it had no inward moisture derived from root nourishment, it withered away.

Is this your case? Is it mine? Have you made quite a show of religion in the flesh, but with no corresponding inner life? Have you understood that growth in the things of God takes place upward and downward at the same time? The Word of God cannot take root on a rocky, unbroken, unsanctified heart.

The attitude to dread more than any other is a form of godliness which has a wonderful show, but no root. If your heart remains unsoftened, the seed of the Word may germinate for a little while, but ultimately—because of lack of moisture, because it has no root and has never gone deep into the well of life which Jesus plants in the heart of a true believer, and there is no response in obedience upon which the Word can fasten—that life withers away. If the mind remains stubborn and the heart unbroken, then any religious experience will die, and judgment is inevitable, because in spite of outward show the fact is that God has never been real. In truth, we have worshiped a dumb idol and have refused to allow God to break our hearts.

Oh, that the Word would plough deep into your soul! Let His Word cast its root down deep into your heart. May He meet no resistance, but rather find a heart that hungers and thirsts for Himself!

I wonder if this has gone home to you who perhaps for years have put up some semblance of a profession of faith, but you have had no root. Today you find your spiritual life withering away, because every time the gospel is preached it strikes the irresistible rock of a mind that rejects Him and of a heart that rebels against Him. What will it take to break such a heart? I know what it took to break mine—a revelation of Calvary and what it must have meant for Christ to bear away my sin.

Here is the final answer, the final contrast of Isaiah 46, where the powerlessness of idols is contrasted with the power of Jehovah. ". . . I will place salvation in Zion for Israel my glory" (v. 13).

Think of those words. The idols could not save, but Jehovah can. In Him there is power for anything in His will.

Of course, this verse anticipates the day when Our God shall set His King in Zion, when Jesus shall reign over all the world. That will be a great day! But it is yet future. Here is something wonderful for me now, where I live, in my home and in my work.

So near does He bring His righteousness that He places salvation in Zion for Israel His glory. To put that into the language of the New Testament, listen to our Lord as He prayed prior to the cross, "And the glory which thou gavest me I have given them. . . . I in them, and thou in me . . ." (John 17:22, 23).

Listen again as He spoke to a little group of bereft disciples as they were going to lose His presence, "I will pray the Father, and he shall give you another Comforter, that he may abide with you for ever. . . . At that day ye shall know that I am in my Father, and ye in me, and I in you" (John 14:16, 20).

Bless the Lord, it happened at Pentecost! "But ye shall receive power, after that the Holy Ghost is come upon you: and ye shall be witnesses unto me . . ." (Acts 1:8). By that transforming power He achieves in us all His purpose, and He calls His people "my glory"—what an amazing thing! The greatest revelation of the power and glory of God in the world today— indeed the only revelation—is the Christian. The only hope both for your life and for the world is that somehow His glory should get in and take possession of you, and begin to shine through to reveal Christ to others.

13

The Sure Road to Peace

O that thou hadst hearkened to my commandments! then had thy peace been as a river, and thy righteousness as the waves of the sea. (Isaiah 48:18)

There is something about the very tone and content of our text that claims immediate attention, for here is a lament from the heart of God. There is a suggestion here that things need not have been what they were if only His people had hearkened to His command. There is a suggestion, too, that this word is not spoken by some ruthless dictator seeking to reap vengeance upon a disobedient people, but by a Father in heaven who has a remedy to meet their need if only they are prepared to fulfill the conditions.

Of course, I am fully aware that this word was spoken primarily to a very insignificant nation, Judah, yet a people for whom God had a very significant purpose, because you will recall that through them was to be born one who was to be our Saviour. But I am deeply convinced that with equal meaning and authority these words are spoken today to the nations and the churches of the world, as well as to your life and mine.

There has never been a time when God's people have not been face to face with a great principle of evil, concentrated perhaps in the social and moral life of a city. Yet whatever it may be, there has always been that same principle, even though perhaps it has taken many different forms throughout history.

151

Always there has been a conflict between the upsurge of human pride—the vainglory of man—and the glory of God. There has always been a conflict between the pride of intellect and, on the other hand, integrity of character, between the planning of some great utopia without God who alone can give anything permanence. This principle is as strong in the world today as when those massive walls of Babylon enclosed their millions, and dominated the whole world.

As I take this passage of Scripture and apply it to your life and mine, to cities and nations, the whole question is, what is our relationship to society? As we live in the midst of it and inevitably mingle with people, what is our attitude? What are we doing, and how are we doing it? I believe we are warranted in applying to present circumstances everything we read here of that which plagued and captivated the people of God, and His exposure of their need, and His great call to deliverance.

I would not presume to suppose that I am here to speak to a nation, but I do presume to speak to a soul, and in so doing I speak to a nation which is simply composed of millions of such. If each one of us were to act upon and respond to this great lament from the heart of God before it is too late, what a dynamic part you and I could have in the liberty and freedom, release and authority of His church!

Let me therefore share with you that which God has spoken to my heart through this portion of His Word, with the earnest prayer that He will yet cause all of us not just to listen, but to hearken and to do, so that what is spoken and written has some relevance to what goes on in our lives. There is no place for a torrent of words that merely tickle our ears and interest our intellects, but a vital need for the authoritative message of God the Holy Spirit for His church at this time, in every department of its life.

As I listen to this lament, and have tried to expose my own life to its message, I have seen some things here that I want to share with you.

In the first place, there is the sadness of a missed responsibility: "O that thou hadst hearkened to my commandments!"

It has been said that man's chief end is to glorify God and not himself. I glorify Him only when I obey Him, not simply when I patronize Him or give some adherence to the church. Yes, I am deeply impressed with the simplicity of the road to revival. Just twenty-four hours' obedience in our lives, and we would be living in such a flood tide of Holy Spirit blessing that there would not be room enough to contain it! Hence this complaint from the Lord, "O that thou hadst hearkened to my commandments!"

Of course, there was nothing new in that. It had been plain from the very beginning of God's dealings with His people that obedience was the key which would unlock the door that would release all the blessing they were capable of receiving, and disobedience was the sure way to lose it. Here is a passage of Scripture for authority for that statement:

"See, I have set before thee this day life and good, and death and evil; In that I command thee this day to love the Lord thy God, to walk in his ways, and to keep his commandments and his statutes and his judgments, that thou mayest live and multiply: and the Lord thy God shall bless thee in the land whither thou goest to possess it. But if thine heart turn away, so that thou wilt not hear, but shalt be drawn away, and worship other gods, and serve them; I denounce unto you this day, that ye shall surely perish, and that ye shall not prolong your days upon the land, whither thou passest over Jordan to go to possess it. I call heaven and earth to record this day against you, that I have set before you life and death, blessing and cursing: therefore choose life, that both thou and thy seed may live" (Deuteronomy 30:15–19).

In case some dispensationalist would say, "This is law and not grace," lest any imagine that this is for the Jew and not for his own heart and life today, let me remind you that the Lord Jesus said, "Not every one that saith unto me, Lord, Lord, shall enter into the kingdom of heaven; but he that doeth the will of my Father which is in heaven. . . . Therefore whosoever heareth these sayings of mine, and doeth them, I will liken him unto a wise man, which built his house upon a rock: And the rain

154 FAITH FOR THE TIMES

descended, and the floods came, and the winds blew, and beat upon that house; and it fell not: for it was founded upon a rock" (Matthew 7:21, 24, 25).

God forgives freely by His grace, but He expects a high performance from the lives of those who have been forgiven. His free forgiveness and His free mercy are offered to us on the terms of simple faith and total commitment to the sovereignty of Jesus Christ, but immediately there is the demand for totality of performance in the power that He gives. "If ye love me, keep my commandments" (John 14:15).

Yes, the one word which opens the door to the outpouring of the blessing of our heavenly Father is *submission,* and the one word which shuts it is *pride.* That is why at the very heart of the Christian revelation there is the cross of Jesus Christ, and that is the place upon which I would ask you to gaze in your soul today: upon Him who humbled Himself and was obedient unto death, and therefore God has highly exalted Him, and given Him a name that is above every name, that at the name of Jesus every knee should bow (Philippians 2:8–10).

Something of the fruit of this obedience is revealed in our text: "O that thou hadst hearkened to my commandments! then had thy peace been as a river, and thy righteousness as the waves of the sea" (Isaiah 48:18).

Peace as a river, not a stream that scarcely fills its little bed, not just a babbling, noisy brook at the beginning of its flow, but a river far down its course like the mighty Amazon, deep and placid. A river, able to bear great tonnage on its surface, carrying in it the garbage of cities and towns and villages. A river, not swept by storm or drained by drought; a deep, mighty, flowing river, never anxious as to whether or not it can continue to flow, giving nourishment to all manner of plants, trees, and shrubs that send their roots deep down into it.

The river speaks of constant fulness and contact with the sinfulest, foulest, and most degraded, yet contact with no contamination. It is a sure, steady, deep flow which gives nourishment not to a few, but to hundreds of lives who seek to draw upon the reality of Jesus Christ within the believer.

". . . and thy righteousness as the waves of the sea." I think (and of course this is only my personal preference) of all God's creation there is nothing I love so much as the ocean. I do not mean the shore at low tide when all is dirty and slimy, but right out in the midst where there is no land in sight, and all around there are great twenty-foot waves crashing onto a ship! I listen to the roar of them, and see their power, and smell their freshness. I see them dancing here and there, and I know that underneath are fathoms of ocean, and the whole thing is so pure, so grand, so powerful!

To many it has not been that way. Peace and righteousness are but a haunting memory because there was failure at one point of obedience. Would you please notice from our text that it was not a question of failure in the practice of religion? To see this in its context, note the first verse, and listen to God launching upon this complaint to His people:

"Hear ye this, O house of Jacob, which are called . . . by the name of the Lord, and make mention of the God of Israel. . . ."

Yes, they do all that, but not in truth nor in righteousness. There has been a very fair show of worship, but it was all an outward thing, and certainly not a matter of the heart, because the Lord says, "I knew that thou art obstinate, and thy neck is an iron sinew, and thy brow brass" (v. 4).

May the Spirit of God drive it into your mind and heart so that there can be no escaping it: basic to the sadness of this missed responsibility was failure to submit to the will and purpose of God. Can you not trace lack of peace and righteousness, of liberty and purity, of power and freshness, to exactly the same source? At some point and on some issue there has been obstinacy; at some place there has been the unbending will and the stubborn mind which would not yield, and insisted on holding on to the reins of life in some situation. Isn't it amazing what the flesh can do in putting on a remarkable show of piety alongside an unbroken will and an unrepentant heart? It is amazing how far we can go inside a casing that is like steel! There was an argument with heaven, and ever since that took place, God has spoken to you about your associations, your friendships, your habits, your practices, your thoughts. Ah, but there was a stubborn obstinancy at that point, and ever since that happened you said goodbye to peace and righteousness, and you forgot it by singing, "It is well with my soul."

As I thought about this my heart felt sad, but God speaks again about what I have called the surety of a merciful redemption. "For my name's sake will I defer mine anger, and for my praise will I refrain for thee, that I cut thee not off. . . . For mine own sake, even for mine own sake, will I do it: for how should my name be polluted? and I will not give my glory unto another" (v. 9, 11).

I do not profess to understand this, I merely make it as a statement because I believe it, and I do believe many things I don't understand! Quite clearly the language is that of One who does not force His will arbitrarily upon His creatures, but rather conditions His treatment of us by our response. How simple and clear is the way by which peace may flow and righteousness sweep over us! Oh, but how long and how hard is the way of rejection! Living my life up to the light I have by His strength, keeping His commandments by His power, and then peace shall be as a river. But if I refuse, something happens that need never happen: "I have refined thee, but not with silver; I have chosen thee in the furnace of affliction" (v. 10).

I want to talk to you about that furnace. Let me be clear about this, that not all suffering is caused by disobedience. The furnace through which I pass in life does not always indicate my unfaithfulness to God. Everyone has some trial or other. There is a skeleton in every cupboard. There is a very big difference between the punishment of the ungodly and the furnace through which God puts His people. Maybe there is a corner around which you are going in life, and I have never been there. There may be a tunnel through which I am passing, and you have never been in it. There is therefore a common bond of sympathy that draws us together because this happens to all.

If, however, you are unfaithful, then you may expect a furnace the like of which the ungodly man knows nothing. If I speak to some young Christian individual who has let go his chastity, God is going to put him through a hell on earth until he repents, a furnace the like of which he has never known a thing about, because he has let go the most cherished thing in life, his own sanctity and chastity. Oh, how many of God's people today are going through a furnace which need never have been, if only they had been willing and obedient!

I do not talk theory, but from my heart and experience. I can recall a time in my life when for almost a year it seemed as if there was a blackout in my soul. I began to talk to others about the wonderful thing of going through darkness and what the Lord has for us then, which is true. I began to speak about the maturity of a Christian, how God can trust him to go alone in the dark, and therefore he does not need to be dependent upon feelings and emotions—perfectly true. I made a scapegoat of some of the greatest truths of Scripture to excuse my sheer, downright disobedience and sin. Has that ever happened to you?

Amid all the cruelty, luxury, and wickedness of Babylon the Jews spent seventy years in slavery that need never have been. But they were God's chosen people, and even though in captivity, His promise never let them go. He could not forget that they belonged to Him. His covenant was made with them, and they could not slip out of His grasp, yet they kicked against His will. But you know, the furnace did its work. They were put into it because of their idolatry, and they came out of it never to worship idols again. The precious thing following their Babylonian captivity was their Scriptures, which they guarded and kept at all costs; never again did they fall before idol worship.

The greatest tragedy is not pain or suffering; it is not the mystery of it all, but the fruitlessness of it, when in spite of the fact that God puts a person through the furnace he hardens his neck, resists, and fails to respond to the fire of affliction.

"Now no chastening for the present seemeth to be joyous, but grievous: nevertheless afterward it yieldeth the peaceable

fruit of righteousness unto them which are exercised thereby"
(Hebrews 12:11).

Are you in a spiritual Babylon? If only you had never taken
that step out of the will of God! How long have you been there?
It took a year for Him to deal with me. How long has He taken
to deal with you?

Has disobedience involved you in the coil of suffering, difficulty, and tragedy from which there seems no escape? Has God
been hammering at your heart daily, and it is as if encased in
steel? One day, if you are a true child of God, you are going to
give in. Don't think you can harden your heart to affliction and
suffering and just go on sinning: that would land you in a lost
eternity, and it would not be God's fault. But if you are a Christian, He is going to have His way with you yet, but it is costing
a high price to His love, to you, and maybe to others.

Ah, but I can tell you that the furnace need not continue.
"For my name's sake . . ." (Isaiah 48:9). Blessed truth! Not for
my merit, not for anything in myself, because the fire and furnace of God's affliction have done their work when they have
brought me to be as dust and ashes. They have burned until
they have left me like that.

Does it seem hard when I tell you that is exactly what God
wants to do with His people, to reduce them to that? He will
not give His glory to another, and when I come to recognize
that, it cannot be by my merit but for His name's sake.

Let submission take the place of stubbornness. Let utter
obedience take the place of rebellion. Let humility take the
place of pride—and you are out of the furnace immediately!

"Thus saith the Lord, thy Redeemer, the Holy One of Israel;
I am the Lord thy God which teacheth thee to profit, which
leadeth thee by the way that thou shouldest go" (v. 17).

There is also here the summons to a mighty recovery: "Go ye
forth of Babylon, flee ye from the Chaldeans, with a voice of
singing declare ye, tell this, utter it even to the end of the earth;
say ye, The Lord hath redeemed his servant Jacob" (v. 20).

The clarion call from the throne of all power and authority
is speaking to the depths of the soul, "Get out from your bond-

age and from under this rebellion; get out!" It was a summons to an exodus. It was a call to separation, and it finds its echo in the call of the Lord to the church in the Book of the Revelation: "Come out of her, my people, that ye be not partakers of her sins, and that ye receive not of her plagues" (Revelation 18:4).

This is not God saying to you, "Give up a few surface habits."

Of course, if you are a Christian and you go on with the Lord, you will not want such hindrances, and that's all.

Rather it is the Lord with the sword of His Word, and with an authority the like of which there is nothing in all the universe, saying to you, "Stop! Get out from your sin of disobedience, and cease enjoying the habits that are sapping your life and dragging you down." Let His sword work until there is soul surgery, down in the depths of your personality.

Not I, but the Lord says to you today, "Go ye forth!" and the Spirit of God with the authority of the Word says, "Come out, let God burn up that spirit of worldly love; come out from fellowship with darkness and evil!"

You know what this means, don't you? That is what makes us afraid.

It would be a dangerous thing to press an argument to a conclusion by saying that before you can help another you have to go through the same experience yourself. I am not here to parade the unsaved days of the man who is preaching, but I tell you, when I heard this alarm bell in my own soul and knew that God called for a holy life from me, and nothing else mattered but an integrity and a transparency that would be right—not by my merit but by His name's sake—I knew that His call must win, and that He must triumph. It was as if I was being pulled out of the quagmire, often against the desire of my own sinful heart, but I was pulled and dragged out of it by a power greater than myself. I was so afraid because I said, "Oh, Lord, if You take me that way, You are going to starve me: I cannot live without this and that! They have become part of my life and character."

It seemed such a desert between Babylon and Jerusalem. But God has said, "They thirsted not when he led them through the deserts: he caused the waters to flow out of the rock for them: he clave the rock also, and the waters gushed out" (Isaiah 48:21).

Has the furnace done its work in your life? God would speak to you now and say, "My child, the time of your discipline is fulfilled; the time of the furnace is over. I want to take the heat and pressure off; I want you to be released and to go free. But I must have your submission, your repentance, and your willingness to let go all that which has forced Me to apply the rod of correction, and the whip of chastisement."

If you are prepared to come to terms with Him, then you will surely know the release once more of the rivers of living water and the satisfying life of Jesus Himself in your heart.